The Spirit-Filled
Church in Action

THE
SPIRIT-FILLED
CHURCH
IN ACTION

*The Dynamics of Evangelism
from the Book of Acts*

A.B. Simpson

Christian Publications
Camp Hill, Pennsylvania

Christian Publications
3825 Hartzdale Drive, Camp Hill, PA 17011

Faithful, biblical publishing since 1883

ISBN: 0-87509-654-9
LOC Catalog Number: 95-83827
©1996 Christian Publications, Inc
All rights reserved
Printed in the United States of America

96 97 98 99 00 5 4 3 2 1

CONTENTS

CHAPTER 1

THE DISPENSATION
OF THE SPIRIT

*He said to them: "It is not for you to know
the times or dates the Father has set by his own
authority. But you will receive power when the
Holy Spirit comes on you; and you will be my
witnesses in Jerusalem, and in all Judea and
Samaria, and to the ends of the earth." (Acts
1:7–8)*

The "Acts of the Apostles" has been variously
called "The Acts of the Holy Spirit" and
"The Acts of the Ascended Lord." Both names are
appropriate, much more appropriate, indeed, than
the more ordinary title of "Acts of the Apostles."
This book records not only the first chapters of
Church history, but the first acts of the Holy
Spirit on earth and the ascended Lord in heaven.

The Perspective

It is important at the very outset that we should
get the right projection of the dispensation of the

Spirit—the perspective, as it were, of faith and hope as it looks out from Christ's ascension to the close of the dispensation and the eternal purpose of God in redemption. In order to do this, there are three points that we must definitely and vividly fix in our thought and conception: first, the departing Lord; secondly, the returning Lord; thirdly, the descending Holy Spirit. These three points stand closely related to each other and can only be rightly understood when viewed in their mutual bearing.

SECTION I—*The Departing Lord*

The opening verses of Acts give us the picture of His ascension.

Foretold His Going

1. This had been definitely foretold by Him. "I came from the Father and entered the world"; again, "I am leaving the world and going back to the Father" (John 16:28), "It is for your good that I am going away. . . . If you loved me, you would be glad that I am going to the Father" (16:7; 14:28). In these and many similar intimations, the Lord had prepared them for His departure, and made them understand that His work on earth was now finished and that His ascension was only part of His great redeeming plan.

Preparations

2. His preparations for the ascension were delib-

erate and complete. He did not go with unseemly haste, but lingered for 40 days, meeting with them often and finishing all that remained of His prophetic ministry on earth before He assumed His priestly and kingly functions in the heavens. "He showed himself to these men and gave many convincing proofs that he was alive" (Acts 1:3). He left no doubt whatever of His identity, and He gave them full instructions concerning the kingdom of God. John tells us that if all the things He said had been recorded, the whole world could not contain the books that should be written. We may be sure then that the practice and example of the apostles, as recorded in the book of Acts, were covered by explicit directions from the Master's lips in messages that have not come to us except as we can infer them from the manner in which the apostles themselves obeyed them.

The Scene

3. The incidents of His departure were most impressive and glorious. Talking with them in His ordinary way, He had led them out as far as Bethany. Then, as if to close the little service, He raised His hands in benediction; but instead of disappearing as was His custom during the 40 days, with a calm, majestic power that neutralized without an effort the law of gravitation, He slowly began to rise before them, while His hands were still outstretched in blessing, His face beaming with love, and His lips, perhaps, still parted with farewell messages, until the vision of His majestic form grew more dis-

tant and dim in the receding space, and at length a floating cloud passed between and received Him out of their sight. Perhaps it was a cloud of angels awaiting Him as His escort. And as they steadfastly gazed, His blessed form appeared no more, but passed up into the heavens, while the next object that claimed their attention was a sudden message from two angelic beings who had dropped from that heavenly company to bring them yet one message more from their loving and departed Lord.

Still the Same

4. His ascension did not change His person or character, for He distinctly sends them word that He is to remain "this same Jesus" (1:11) until they shall see Him again on His more glorious return. So in heaven where He dwells, He is still the old Christ of Galilee and Bethany, as human, as loving, as near to the race with whom He has become forever identified.

> Though now ascended upon high,
> He bends on earth a brother's eye;
> Partaker of the human name,
> He knows the frailty of our frame.
>
> In every pang that rends the heart
> The Man of Sorrows has a part;
> He sympathizes with our grief,
> And to the sufferer sends relief.

Still Working

5. His ascension did not terminate His work, for

Luke tells his friend, Theophilus, that his former treatise related only to those things which Jesus "began to do and to teach" (Acts 1:1). His present treatise, therefore, by inference, is to relate to the things which Jesus will continue to do and teach. Jesus' ascension simply introduces another stage of His ministry. Now He officiates as our great High Priest and our sovereign Lord and King. Girded for constant service, He ever appears in the presence of God for us, and governs the universe with unceasing power and wisdom, as Head over all things for His body, the Church. Not for a moment is He idle or occupied with His own happiness. His ascension was as unselfish as His crucifixion, and He is finishing His glorious work and preparing the kingdom which He is soon to reveal to His waiting Bride.

Where Is Heaven?

Where did He go when He rose that day into the blue dome of heaven? While, undoubtedly, heaven is a character and state, it is just as surely also a place. There the real body of our living Lord resides, and there with Him are the actual spirits of the just made perfect, real subsistences and not ghostly shadows; persons who dwell somewhere and have a home as real as the earth they left. But which of yonder glorious worlds was the goal of that glorious journey? Was it the mighty "Arcturus and his sons," that mightiest sun in yonder ether; or was it one of those marvelous systems which astronomy has revealed, where two suns revolve in their heavens, and while one has sunk beneath the horizon the other rises to its meridian and there is no night there? Or was it to one of those celestial empires where a group of colored suns sheds a radiance so glorious as to turn every object on which their light might fall into a flashing gem of untold beauty? Or was it one of those brilliant star clusters where the eye of the telescope can discern a thousand suns in a single system? Whither did He go from Bethany that day and where is the home of the ascended Lord? Is it possible to find an answer to our eager questions from these pages of revelation?

Above All Heavens

There is one passage which tells us that he "ascended higher than all the heavens, in order to fill the whole universe" (Ephesians 4:10). Surely, that means that there is a sense in which all those glorious suns and stars are at His feet and around His throne, and yet that somehow He fills all the empires where their light and power extend with His presence and His actual consciousness. May this not be true? We know that the telephone and the telescope have practically annihilated distance, the one bringing the voices of the remotest regions to our side, the other bringing the distant heavenly bodies right into our immediate view. Now, suppose that in yonder heavenly world the inhabitants should have in their own brains, their ears, their eyes, their refined and perfect physical senses, all the powers of the telescope and the telephone, and this would not be hard; then, from that heavenly throne you could look out and see the most distant stars as if they were just at hand, and hear the farthest voices of the universe as distinctly as you hear the friend that is talking by your side. And thus all things would be gathered into unity together, and all the luminaries of the heavens become the lamps that light up the palace of the King, and all the voices of every planet and star one sublime harmony, one celestial chorus, ever rising in symphonies divine, and saying, as John heard every creature that was in heaven and in earth and under the earth saying, "To him who sits on the throne and to the Lamb/ be praise and honor and glory and power, for ever and ever!" (Revelation 5:13). If that is heaven, oh, how glorious it must be! Doubtless, that is the power Christ possesses now, and that makes it as easy for Him to bend His ear to our faintest cry as if He were still at Bethany. And that is the power which we one day shall share with Him when we behold His glory and shall be like Him, when we see Him as He is. Then we shall thank Him for His ascension just as much as for His lowly incarnation and His dying love.

SECTION II—*The Returning Lord*

His Coming

1. But now upon our vision is projected another picture just as necessary to complete the conception of God's perfect plan. It is the picture of the returning Lord. He had just disappeared from their view,

and they were in danger of thinking that He had gone forever; therefore, it is necessary to arouse them by another vision. And so, as they intently watch the distant and receding cloud, lo, two shining angels stand beside them, who speak to them as visitors from another world: "Men of Galilee, . . . why do you stand here looking into the sky? This same Jesus, who has been taken from you into heaven, will come back in the same way you have seen him go into heaven" (Acts 1:11).

Just as when you have been sailing out of the harbor of New York on a distant ocean voyage, you have just said farewell to that beloved group on the dock and have seen their forms and faces and waving handkerchiefs fade in the dim distance, while your eyes grew more dim with tears, and suddenly you have been recalled to yourself by the steward telling you to get ready to send ashore whatever mail you had to give the pilot at Sandy Hook, and you realized that you had time to send one more parting message to your friends, and that brief but loving word was swiftly penned and sealed and sent, and in it you compressed your last and best message of love, until you should come again yourself. So the Lord was sailing out of the harbor of the terrestrial atmosphere into the great ocean of space, and He tarried a moment on the way to send these two angelic messengers with one more word of love. But that word, how important! For it was to mark the goal of all their future hopes and expectations, and to reveal something even more glorious than all He had taught them hitherto, namely: that His going away was but the prelude to His coming back again, and that the one key to all the problems of life, the one remedy for all the wrongs of time, the one solution of all the question of truth, the one outlook of faith and the one supreme goal of hope, was to be this blessed prospect and promise of His own literal and visible return.

But first He tells them that He is coming back actually and literally. It is not to be fulfilled in their death or their closer union with Him, by the coming of the Holy Spirit or the spreading of His kingdom on earth, but He Himself is coming, and all the rest is but a preparation for the King.

2. He tells them that they shall see Him come. "This same Jesus . . . will come back in the same way you have seen him go into heaven" (1:11). It will be visible, personal and beyond all possible mistake or confusion.

3. It will be the same Jesus that will come, arrayed, no doubt, in the majesty of the Father, the glory of the angels and the forces of the universe. He will still have the same form, the same face, the same loving heart, and we will know Him as our brother and our Christ. Our hearts will instantly and instinctively recognize Him and reach out to Him in the presence of His majesty, even as we do when He comes to dwell in the heart, its welcome Guest.

4. He will come as He went away. And how did He go away? He went away blessing them, with His hands extended in benediction. So will He

come again with those arms stretched out in greeting to welcome us to His breast. Oh, not in terror, not in judgment, not as the dread Avenger is Jesus coming! Banish from your hearts these unscriptural and unbelieving specters. It is the Bridegroom that is coming. Let us love His appearing. Let us be preparing to welcome Him with joy and not with grief.

This, then, is the goal of prophecy and the outlook of faith. Now place these two points clearly in your spiritual view like the two centers of a great ellipse, and you will be prepared for the next point.

SECTION III—*The Descending Holy Spirit*

His Relation to Christ's Coming

The Holy Spirit comes, not to be the final factor in the Christian dispensation, but as a temporary administration: first, to finish Christ's earthly work, and secondly, to prepare the way for His second coming. But we are not prepared to understand the coming of the Spirit until we first see these two clear points—the departing and returning Lord—and between them, like a parenthesis, the dispensation of the Holy Spirit to follow the one and herald the other. The business therefore, of the Holy Spirit, and the Church through which He operates, is to bring Christ back again, and so to complete the ministry which He began on earth that He can come to bring its final stage in the setting up of His millennial kingdom on the very place where He was rejected and crucified.

Having understood this, the place of the Spirit's dispensation, let us look at the promise of the Spirit as given us by the departing Lord.

A Person

1. He was to be a Person as real as Christ Himself. It is not something that we receive from God in this deeper life, but Somebody who comes to make Himself known to us, to make Himself real to us and to be in us the source of all strength and happiness.

Power

2. He was to come as the Spirit of power. Man is the weakest of beings, weaker than his own sinful nature, weaker than the elements around him, weaker even than the brutes over whom he was sent to exercise dominion. But the Holy Spirit comes to give him power, to make his life effectual, and when the Holy Spirit comes into our life He does something. He accomplishes something. He is more than a sentiment, a feeling, a fancy. He is an infinite force that makes our life powerful and enables us to accomplish all for which we are called as the disciples of Christ. It is power over sin, power over self, power over the world, power over sickness, power over Satan, power to be, to do, to suffer and to overcome.

In Us

3. The Holy Spirit does not work apart from us.

The Master died and trod the wine press alone, single-handed, and went to the dragon's den and destroyed him. But the Holy Spirit is not like Christ. We are His temple. He resides in us and works through us, and unless we yield ourselves to be His instruments, He is unable to carry out His supreme purposes, and the great exalted Head is like a man with a paralyzed body that refuses to perform the functions for which that brain has power sufficient, but the paralyzed members are unequal to the effort. Therefore, the Spirit claims us as the subjects of His working.

Witnesses

4. The Spirit's power is to be shown chiefly in our witnessing for Christ. That is the form of our service. We are not to witness of truth merely, not to become wise and wonderful orators or teachers, but we are to be witnesses of Him. I do not know how to express this better than to say that our business is to make Jesus real to men, so to live and so to speak that they shall see in us and through us a power and a Presence that will make them long for the same loving and almighty help in their lives. Thus to minister Christ to men is the highest service to which we can be called, and the most helpful thing we can do for weak and erring men.

Aggressive Work

5. The sphere of their ministry was to be an ever-expanding one: "in Jerusalem, and in all Judea and

Samaria, and to the ends of the earth" (1:8). Of course, we cannot now stop to follow this widening circle as the apostolic Church followed it through their great missionary campaign until the whole inhabited world had received the message of Christ. This remarkable verse is just a table of contents of the whole book of Acts, and the chapters that follow are the best commentary upon it, as successively we see the gospel planted first in Jerusalem, then throughout all Judea, next in Samaria and finally in the remotest heathen nations.

Doubtless, also, we have here a hint for the individual Christian, of the Spirit-filled life and service that will always begin at home, our Jerusalem; and then reach out to our relatives ("all Judea"); and next find its way to our very enemies, those farther removed from us and having, perhaps, no natural claim upon us—Samaria; and then finally will lead us out in sympathy and service to be in some sense missionaries to the very heathen lands and send the gospel to the uttermost part of the earth.

Tarry

6. They were to tarry for this baptism of power. Without it they must not attempt their work, nor must we. If the Lord Himself would not begin His earthly ministry until He had received the baptism of the Holy Spirit, how much less dare we presume to go forth in our own strength and represent Him!

Why should they need to tarry? First, perhaps

because the fullness of the time must first come, and the Pentecostal hour which, according to the Hebrew calendar, was to be interpreted and fulfilled in the coming of the Spirit, should have arrived. But secondly, and doubtless much more probably, because they themselves were not ready, and the waiting days were necessary for their spiritual preparation, to bring them to the end of themselves, to show them their need, to give them time to search their hearts, to deepen the hunger and the longing which were necessary for them to appreciate the blessing and to make full room and right of way in their hearts for His indwelling and outworking.

And so let us wait for the promise of the Father. Let us receive in all His fullness the blessed Holy Spirit; and if any reader has not yet proved this promise true, be encouraged, dear friend, to follow even the dim light that is now shining in your heart, even the faintest longing that is springing in your soul. No words that we could speak would make you understand this experience until it comes to you. If there is within you a sense of something that you need and do not have—a cry for God in some way to give you purity, victory, power and rest—that is the blessing already begun. If you follow on to know the Lord, then surely will you know Him. He would never give you that longing desire and disappoint it when you came to tarry at His feet. Wait for the promise of the Father, "Seek the LORD while he may be found;/ call on him while he is near" (Isaiah 55:6), and "you will receive power when the Holy Spirit comes on you; and you will be my witnesses in Jerusalem, and in all Judea and Samaria, and to the ends of the earth" (Acts 1:8).

CHAPTER 2

PENTECOSTAL POWER

These men are not drunk, as you suppose. It's only nine in the morning! No, this is what was spoken by the prophet Joel:

> *"In the last days, God says,*
> *I will pour out my Spirit on all people.*
> *Your sons and daughters will prophesy,*
> *your young men will see visions,*
> *your old men will dream dreams."*
> *Acts 2:15–17)*

We have glanced at the great points that were to mark the beginning and close of the Christian age, the departing and the returning Lord, and touched upon the great event that stands between these two—the coming of the Holy Spirit to administer the dispensation until the Lord Jesus shall come again. The Holy Spirit was to fulfill the work that Christ left undone and to prepare the way for the greater work which Christ Himself is coming back some day to complete. The great theme of the Acts of the Apostles is the Holy Spirit's coming and the power which He was to bring.

The Importance of His Coming

1. Let us look first at the event itself, its magnitude, its stupendous importance and far-reaching power. What was it? It was something like the difference between the reign of David and the reign of Solomon. David came to lay the foundation for the work which Solomon followed to fulfill. When David had made his preparations he passed out of view and Solomon came to complete the work and rear that splendid temple. And so Jesus Christ in His earthly ministry had prepared the way for the building of His Church, the spiritual temple. Now He withdraws for a season from the scene, and the Holy Spirit comes to erect the edifice of the Church of God out of living stones. When this is done Jesus will come again to enter His temple and reign over it, even as David is coming back again in the millennial age to sit once more upon his throne.

The event which this book of Acts records is nothing less than the actual descent of the Deity to this globe, the coming of the third Person of the Godhead, on a visitation of 2,000 years to one of the smallest orbs of space. It is a stupendous event. Jesus came to visit it as the Son of God for 33 years. Here we have a Divine Person just as great as Jesus—the Holy Spirit— leaving heaven, for He is no longer a resident there, and making His home on earth for 2,000 years. As a missionary might go to some leper hospital, to some outcast race, to some scene of barbarism and degradation, and, with his refinement and culture and higher tastes, settle down among these people and spend his lifetime—so this gentle, glorious Being, the Spirit of God, the Mind that made every mind in the universe, that garnished the heavens, made the beautiful stars, the glories of earth and all things that are lovely—the Holy Spirit—the Intelligence, the Executive of the Godhead, actually left heaven and moved down to this little planet and has been living upon it, making it His headquarters ever since that Pentecostal day.

What Was The Difference Of Pentecost?

What was the difference between the Holy Spirit's coming and His Old Testament manifestations? In the Old Testament He only came to certain persons, prominent leaders, to men called to be prophets or priests or kings and perform some distinguished service. He came to such and gave them special qualifications for their work. He did not come to the great mass of people. There is no single example of a slave or a person of lower stage in the Old Testament being filled with the Holy Spirit. Now we are told He will come to all flesh, even the handmaidens and slaves without distinction of sex, rank or education. In the Old Testament the Holy Spirit came upon them. On this day of Pentecost He came in them. He was with them, but now He enters and becomes part of the inner life of the one in whom He dwells. It is a presence not with us, but in us.

Then again the Holy Spirit comes to us now for witnessing and service. The Jewish dispensation knew nothing of this. Their business was to keep the light among themselves and be exclusive and separate from the Gentiles. It is all different now. The Holy Spirit comes to spread the light, to make every man a reflector, a messenger and witness of Jesus Christ, and to expand and distribute this glorious gospel until it shall reach the uttermost parts of the earth.

Then again the Holy Spirit often came upon a bad man like Saul, yet did not change Saul's heart. He did not make Balaam a holy man. He gave power to these men for a purpose and an occasion. The Holy Spirit now comes to good men and to make men good. He comes for moral cleansing and quickening. He will not dwell in a heart that is willfully unholy.

Once again, the Holy Spirit differs in this age from the past because He comes now as the Spirit of Jesus. In the Old Testament He came as the Deity, the Spirit of the Father, distant and mighty. Now He comes as the Spirit of the Son, as the gentle heart of Jesus, the One that wept in His tears, loved in His tenderness, suffered in His pains, sympathized in His compassion. Now the Holy Spirit is the very embodiment and expression of the love and sweetness of the Christ of Galilee.

The Time of His Coming

2. The day of Pentecost was the time He chose

for His descent. It was a special day. He did not vaguely drift into time, but there was a line of demarcation, a point of contact, an instant when He entered this planet and settled in this world as His abiding home. There are reasons why He should not have come before. There were reasons why He should come then. The day of Pentecost was a Jewish feast of little interest to the Gentiles, but intensely interesting to Israel. Their ecclesiastical year was divided into 12 months, seven calendar months and five left blank because God did not give them a full plan of all the ages. The rest is to be filled up when He comes again. The ecclesiastical year began with the Passover, which stands for Calvary, where all our eras begin. Then came Pentecost in the next month. That is the second chapter of Church history. The Holy Spirit comes after Calvary also in the individual experience. Later came the Feast of Trumpets implying testimony for Christ, the Day of Atonement and the Feast of Tabernacles in the seventh month representing the coming of the Lord. The Feast of Pentecost was specially the one which celebrated the beginning of their harvest. The Feast of Tabernacles represented the full harvest.

Then Pentecost was also the anniversary of the law. It was on that very day that Moses gathered Israel around Mount Sinai, God came out in majesty and gave His law with His thunders and lightnings and they stood trembling and entered into the covenant of works with Him. Now the Holy Spirit comes on that anniversary because the

Holy Spirit is the new law of the Christian. The old law was written on stone. The new law is written on the tablets of the heart. The old law was outside, while the new law is put within you as an instinct and intuition of your being, something that is part of your very nature.

"I will make a new covenant/ with the house of Israel. . . . This is the covenant . . . I will put my law in their minds/ and write it on their hearts./ I will be their God,/ and they will be my people" (Jeremiah 31:31, 33). Therefore, the Holy Spirit came on the anniversary of the law that He might be to us, instead of the words of Sinai, the mere sense of duty which will never make anybody good.

Pentecost was the feast of the first harvest—so the Holy Spirit comes to bring the first harvest of the earth. That is the key to the whole missionary question. God is not saving the world, but He is saving the first sheaves out of the world. We are sent, not to convert everybody, but to gather out of the nations a people for His name.

We must not wonder if nine out of every 10 refuse the gospel. We must not be disappointed if results seem limited. It is a selective age, only every man makes the selection for himself. God gives everybody the call, and "all who were appointed for eternal life believed" (Acts 13:48). God sends us to gather samples of the nations, and do not think that God is disappointed or the Holy Spirit is baffled if the great mass of our countrymen are going on the broad road to ruin. They have been going and will keep on going all through the dispensation of the Holy Spirit. Pentecost is the gospel of first fruits.

There is another beautiful thing about this. In Leviticus 23, God is describing the way they are to keep the Passover and also the Feast of Pentecost. He tells them that in the Passover they are to eat unleavened bread because it represents the spotless Lamb of God, leaven standing for human imperfection. After the Passover they had a wave offering of a sheaf, marking the first sheaf of harvest. Then they counted 50 days to Pentecost, and when that came it was celebrated by two loaves waved and also given to God for His food. But those loaves were baked with leaven, the only instance where leaven was allowed in the Levitical ceremony. Why? Surely it teaches that the Holy Spirit would not stay away from us even if we were still poor, imperfect disciples; that the Holy Spirit would come to Peter with his imperfection, and to Thomas with his doubting heart. In other words, you don't need to wait until you are faultless and sinless to receive the Holy Spirit. There is a kind of teaching about sanctification, telling people they must get sanctified and all right themselves, and then the Holy Spirit will come. If you can get ready for the Holy Spirit without Him, you can get along without Him afterward. You have to have Him to make you ready and to make you right. You must have Him come down to where you are, "outside the camp" (Hebrews 13:11–13), and take you in. It is He that sanctifies, and sanctification is not a man all cleaned up himself and saying, "Blessed Holy Spirit, I am all right and I will be glad to have Your company." It is your coming as a poor leper and handing yourself over to Him. The Holy Spirit will take a poor sinner just as graciously as the Savior. And He will never leave you until He has you white and spotless, "without stain or wrinkle or any other blemish" (Ephesians 5:27). That is the meaning of the old Levitical Feast of Pentecost where the loaves had the leaven in them; but God took them and undertook to take the leaven out of them. Don't wait until you have yourself adjusted; come as you are. Take Him to be the First and the Last, for "he is able also to save them," from the uttermost, "to the uttermost that come unto God by him" (Hebrews 7:25, KJV).

Their Preparation for His Coming

3. There was preparation for this great event. "When the day of Pentecost came, they were all together in one place" (Acts 2:1). Rotherham translates it thus: "While the day of Pentecost was being filled up they were all in one place with one object." They were not there at the moment only. They came all the week and were ready because they had been there. It wasn't keeping appointments with God and just sparing one hour out of seven days for His service. It was a time of daily waiting. They were there 10 days and were ready, and that was why He came. They were "all in one place with one object." They took pains to get

everything fixed up. They had a sort of house-cleaning. Some think Peter was all right in proposing to elect an apostle in place of Judas. It seems, however, as if God ignored Peter's apostle. You never hear of him again. He paid no attention to this new apostle, but He chose Paul a little later when he was ready. John speaks of only 12 apostles of the Lamb in Revelation. Peter tried to get everything adjusted. God help us to do the same.

Supernatural Signs of His Coming

4. There were some signs and accompaniments of His coming. We are told there was some kind of a sound, "a sound like the blowing of a violent wind" (Acts 2:2). There was no wind, but the sound of a wind. A little later we are told, "when this was noised abroad" (2:6, KJV), literally, "when the people heard the sound they came running together." There was some strange supernatural voice, some supernatural demonstrations which they and all Jerusalem heard.

It was like wind. Wind is one of the tokens and symbols of the Spirit. Wind, with its tremendous force, so destructive and often so helpful, stands for the Holy Spirit, the mightiest of powers.

Again the symbol of fire is implied in the tongues which sat upon them.

They seem to have appeared like intoxicated men. They were lifted by a divine stimulus to a higher plane. So the apostle says, "Do not get drunk on wine. . . . Instead, be filled with the Spirit" (Ephesians 5:18).

Further the tongues suggest that it was their voices He was to change and use.

Effects of His Coming

5. There were the effects of His coming. It was in general supernatural power. He came to give them a force stronger than sin, disease, Satan or the spirit of popular opinion and the willfulness of the human will, power to make things move; to lift this world and place it in its true orbit around the throne of God. Let us look at these signs of power.

a. The Gift of Tongues

This was the first of the Pentecostal signs and the first to disappear.

b. Power of Testimony

It was not merely the voice, but the message that they spoke had strange power in it. They told about Jesus, His resurrection and coming, and many were stirred, convicted and saved. If you have received the Holy Spirit you are able to speak for God, perhaps not magnificent words, but loving, living words.

c. Power of Conviction

Again it was the power of supernatural conviction, a power that rested on the audience quite apart from the power in the message or the speaker. This is the greatest mark of the Holy Spirit's presence. Oh, for the power that brings people face to face with God, and holds them by a spell that we may not see, but God sees. Ask God for the power of conviction, so that every time the voice of the gospel is uttered there shall be stricken hearts, even as we are told of them that many were cut to the heart and said, "Brothers, what shall we do" (Acts 2:37)?

Will you look for that kind of power; and when you hear no shouts or tears, take the mighty God to move upon the people as a great electric current that will thrill them to their consciences and bring them to their knees? It is power from on high. Not power from the man, but power that comes from God every time.

d. Power of Supernatural Boldness

The men were awed when they saw the boldness of these timid, uneducated fishermen, and they marveled and said, "these men had been with Jesus" (4:13). They had courage and authority to speak, knowing God is behind.

e. Power of Healing

We find right away the power of the Spirit began to touch men's bodies, and the next morning the lame man at the gate Beautiful sprang to his feet leaping and praising God because the Holy Spirit had come. Then each new stage was marked by some manifestation of healing. When they went to Samaria the people were healed and the attention of the multitude was attracted. Peter went to Joppa and Lydda and the people there were healed. Then Paul started out on his missionary journey and the people were healed all along the way. Each new stage seemed to be marked with a new manifestation of the healing power of God.

f. Power of Holiness

Best of all was the power of holiness, for the Holy Spirit does not come to make men great, but He comes to make you real and true first, and then let your life reflect its reality and power on others. Therefore we are told "much grace was upon them all" (4:33). Their lives were beautiful. There was power over selfishness and sin and there was the power of love.

> Every day they continued to meet together in the temple courts. They broke bread in their homes and ate together with glad and sincere hearts, praising God and enjoying the favor of all the people. (2:46–47)

No one could say a word against them. "No one claimed that any of his possessions was his own" (4:32). God taught the Jews all through the Old Testament that property was a sign of God's blessing, prosperity in temporal things was the sign of God's approval, and there was no instinct so strong in the Jews as that of possession. But now they reckoned themselves as trustees, holding it for God. That was power, and it is real still when it works that way. If your consecration and blessing have not opened your purse strings and made it a joy to give to God you have not much of the Holy Spirit.

Communism was established at Pentecost. It was simply the overflow of hearts in a beautiful spectacle of unselfishness. Later all the social boundaries were recognized and Peter clearly intimated that every man had a right to do with his money as he wished. Communism is not, therefore, Christianity. Back of it is the bigger thing— love that gives up your rights when anybody else is wronged by your rights. Love is the law of the New Testament, and while love does not lead to communism, it will lead to sacrifice and live out John Wesley's famous sermon on practical love, which was:

1. Get all you can.
2. Save all you can.
3. Give all you can.

g. Power of Guidance

Again, it was the power of guidance, the power that led men in the right way. You can trace this through the Acts of the Apostles. See Him leading Philip to the desert to meet the eunuch. So He will lead you to the mission field. See Him leading Paul on that marvelous journey to Rome when everything conspired to stop him. A man with his hand in the hand of God, a woman grasping infinite power and wisdom as her protection, is safe. The Holy Spirit is strong enough to lead you safely and will not leave you until He has done all that He has spoken of.

h. Power of Providence

There is nothing that impresses one more in this book of Acts than the power of providence; that is, the power of the Holy Spirit in men's hearts to change circumstances. If God is on the throne inside your heart, as you go forth the winds and waves obey Him and the passions of men subside, the perils of earth and hell fall back and you live a charmed life because the Holy Spirit is upon the throne. You will find this all in the Acts of the Apostles. We see Peter in prison and the curtain falls on the darkest drama. Tomorrow is Passover and the appetite of the brutal mob is whetted for a feast, for Herod has told them they shall have Peter's blood. But God had not been consulted. Oh, how mighty that little "but" in the beginning of the chapter. "Peter was kept in prison, but the church was earnestly praying to God for him" (12:5). At midnight the prison door swung open and a shining guide is by the side of Peter, and he goes forth into liberty. Before yonder sun goes down Herod is seized with an awful pain and dies convulsed in terrible agony.

Many a time since has God worked the same. There was a day when the Sultan of Turkey said that on that very day Christianity should be banished from his dominion, and every Christian found without having recanted must be put to death. But on that very day, less than a century ago, there was a strange panic yonder in Constan-

tinople, for the Sultan was dying, and ere the sun
went down on that fated day the Sultan was dead.
The heart that is filled with the Holy Spirit can
walk safely amid arrows and whirlwinds and
death, for "in all things God works for the good of
those who love him, who have been called according to his purpose" (Romans 8:28).

i. Power to Suffer

Finally there is power to suffer, power to be
sweet amid wrong and persecution, to stand like
Stephen when they gnashed upon him with their
teeth, and made them gnash the more when they
saw his face like an angel and they dared not look
upon him, power like him to say, "Lord, do not
hold this sin against them" (Acts 7:60). That was
the mightiest power of the Holy Spirit, a power to
be gently victorious even in suffering and to stand
with the Master in the garden and judgment hall.

j. Power of Salvation

But we must close the picture. Perhaps the most
glorious power of all was the power of salvation,
for Peter, quoting that prophecy of Joel, says,
"And everyone who calls/ on the name of the Lord
will be saved" (2:21). When the Holy Spirit comes
it is so easy to be saved. If you are not saved, come
while the door is open and the Lord is nigh. You
have only to call. The work is done. Salvation is
ready. The Spirit is here.

We have spoken about the earlier experiences of
the Holy Spirit. There is not time to dwell on the

fact that there were several later outpourings of the Spirit even in Pentecostal times. So He is not exhausted when He first comes. But, dear child of God, He has many times of refreshing for you. Have you got your baptism for today? Have you got the filling of the Spirit? He will come to the leavened loaf, but, oh, He comes to take the leaven out and sanctify you wholly and fill you so full that there will be no room for self, the world or sin. God help you to take it in His way.

Once again, the baptism of the Holy Spirit was not meant for higher Christians only. Peter says, "Repent and be baptized, every one of you, in the name of Jesus Christ for the forgiveness of your sins. And you will receive the gift of the Holy Spirit" (2:38). It is for the youngest Christian, and indeed, no soul should leave the altar of salvation until it has been sealed with the Spirit and taught to say:

> Let the water and the blood,
> From Thy riven side which flowed,
> Be of sin the double cure,
> Cleanse me from its guilt and power.

CHAPTER 3

GOD'S PLAN FOR THE AGE

You will be my witnesses in Jerusalem, and in all Judea and Samaria, and to the ends of the earth. (Acts 1:8)

We have already seen that this remarkable verse is an epitome of the whole book of Acts. Were we to express in three words the design and contents of this story of primitive Christianity, those words would be the perspective, the power and the plan of the christian age.

The Perspective

First, we have the perspective given in the first 11 verses of the Acts of the Apostles. Perspective is the relation of objects to each other in the line of vision. The book of Acts gives us the outlook of Christian faith and hope. In its true perspective four great promontories stand out. First the cross, expressed by the word "suffering" in the opening verses of Acts—"his suffering" (1:3). Next is His resurrection and ascension described so vividly in the same passage. Now His cross would not have had the same meaning if it had been looked at alone. It could have signified only death, disaster and utter despair. But when looked at with the resurrection in perspective just beyond, it becomes a stepping stone to glory and victory. Next comes the ascension, but this would have only meant separation from His loving disciples had it not been for the third object that meets our view, namely, the descent of the Holy Spirit, the Comforter, who came to take His place and fill the void of His absence. But even the dispensation of the Holy Spirit is not final. This has been the great mistake of the Church, to look upon it as the end of the Christian age. There looms beyond a still more sublime vision, namely the return of the Lord Jesus, the message of the angels to the bereaved disciples: "This same Jesus . . . will come back in the same way you have seen him go into heaven" (1:11). Thus, as we look at all together, they have upon each other the most vital bearing, and the whole truth is necessary in order rightly to understand each part of the whole.

The Power

Next, the word power expresses that deep underlying truth that runs through the entire book of Acts, impressing us with the fact of a supernatural Person in the bosom of the Church, the power of the Holy Spirit as the heart of Christianity, while Jesus on the throne is its Head. The whole story of primitive Christianity is supernatural. There is no rational explanation for the sudden and widespread movement that brought into the bosom of the Church the men that crucified the Lord and the bitter enemy that pursued Stephen to his death and afterward ravaged the Church of God in the name of religious zeal. The triumphs of the gospel were miracles of grace and power, and the same power must still be recognized or we shall cease to have a living Christianity.

The Plan

But we have already followed these thoughts and facts in some measure, at least, through their unfolding in this history; and so we come to the third of these great outline words: the plan according to which this mighty and divine Person was to evolve the Church and prepare for the coming of the Lord. This is also most clearly given in our text and as clearly unfolded through the entire book. The movement was to begin at Jerusalem, and so we find the earlier chapters of Acts describing the origin, growth and constitution of the Church in Jerusalem. Next it was to reach the scattered Jews throughout all Judea. And so we find the story expanding in the evangelistic work of Peter and Paul among their countrymen scattered abroad. Then Samaria was to be reached, and so the eighth chapter of Acts introduces us to the gospel in Samaria, and late references continue the story. But the final and supreme triumph of Christianity in the Christian age was to be in the remoter realms of heathenism. And so the last half of the book of Acts, from the 13th chapter, is chiefly occupied with the origin and growth of foreign missions and the spread of the gospel to the "ends of the earth" (1:8). Such was the plan of campaign given by the Master and faithfully followed by His first field officers; and such is still the divine order for the Church of God in the aggressive work of Christianity—or, at least, such it ought to be—and only as we follow this plan will we have the Master's approval and blessing. Let us follow in detail these successive stages of aggressive Christianity.

SECTION I—*Jerusalem*

The Church in Jerusalem

This picture occupies the opening pages of Acts. Some striking features of this primitive Church are well worthy of our imitation.

1. It was born upon its knees. It came into being at Pentecost in the spirit and atmosphere of prayer.

2. It was baptized as soon as it was born. Its youngest members were taught to receive the Holy Spirit the moment they had accepted Jesus. "Repent and be baptized, every one of you, in the name of Jesus Christ for the forgiveness of your sins. And you will receive the gift of the Holy Spirit" (2:38). So still we should lead the convert to the altar of consecration and never leave him until he has been sealed and sanctified by the same Spirit and saved from backsliding and defeat.

3. It was a household of love. Joy, praise, mu-

tual affection, self-sacrifice, consideration for others, the care of the poor and the stranger, and the spirit of gladness and love made it a center of attraction and a blessed home circle which drew to it the sad and hungry world, as it still will draw men if it has the same Pentecostal spirit.

4. It was not without a very heart-searching discipline. The incident of Ananias and Sapphira left an awful lesson of the holiness of God and the sin and folly of trifling with His grace; and great fear, as well as great joy, fell upon the infant Church.

5. It had its baptism of fire in the martyrdom of Stephen and James, the imprisonment of Peter and the cruel hatred of Herod and the Jews. And so still, if we have anything worth attacking, the devil will attack it, and if we have anything worth hating, the world will hate it as much as in the days of old.

6. It was scattered abroad by trial, that it might sow the seed in wider fields. When its members were in danger of clinging too closely to their congenial home circle, the Lord had to send them forth by persecution and kindle the fire on other altars.

7. But at length it became established and settled, and "It was strengthened; and encouraged by the Holy Spirit, it grew in numbers, living in the fear of the Lord" (9:31b).

Our Jerusalem

They were first commanded to begin at Jerusalem; and so, when we receive the Holy Spirit, our first witness should be at home in the family circle, to husband or wife, children or parents, brothers and sisters. In the church where God has placed us we should make the name of Jesus felt as "the aroma of Christ among those who are being saved and those who are perishing" (2 Corinthians 2:15). We are not justified in running away from our kindred or even from our Christian associates because they do not agree with us and are not congenial to us. We are to stay until we have finished the testimony and learned the lesson God has for us. Have we been true to those at home, or have we found it harder to live and witness for Christ in these closer circles of love and intimacy than from some public pulpit or to some company of strangers?

SECTION II—*Judea*

The Church Among the Scattered Jews

God has distributed the children of Abraham by many vicissitudes and providences in all parts of the world. They formed a little nucleus in almost every important center of commercial life and became a starting point for the apostolic missions in almost every land. Peter was chiefly their apostle, and we find him going down to Lydda and Joppa, while it is significantly added that he "traveled about the country" (Acts 9:32). Later he seems to be writing from Babylon, where we know there were some 70,000 Jews residing. We know also that there were many Jews in Rome, for we read in Acts of a decree banishing the Jews from Rome, in consequence of which Aquila and Priscilla and others were driven forth to Corinth. Paul also ministered much to his own countrymen and had an insatiable longing, amounting even to self-sacrifice, for their salvation (see Romans 9:3). James writes to them as "the twelve tribes scattered among the nations" (James 1:1), and there seems to have been an understanding that these scattered Jews were not merely remnants of the two tribes of Judah and Benjamin, but that they represented all the 12 tribes of the dispersion. If this be so, the recent theory which has been widely propagated in favor of the identity of the 10 tribes with the Anglo-Saxons, is, of course, without foundation, and the 10 tribes form part of the mass of Hebrews scattered among all nations still. To the Jews, therefore, everywhere the gospel was to be presented first, and this is still its message and its scope. The Gentile portion of the Christian Church has largely forgotten its sacred trust to Christ's kindred according to the flesh. This duty is not entirely fulfilled when we seek out the Jews separately and try to form our class missions for them as a race distinctively, as though they were scarcely fit to be included in our Christian congregations. Surely, this is a mistake. Why should we not preach to them in our common congregations just as directly as to the Gentiles? Why should we know either Jew or Gentile in the one Church of Jesus Christ? Why should we not seek and expect to attract them as hearers of the gospel in all our places of worship, and receive them to equal membership and love in all our Christian fellowships? Surely, this is the intention of the apostolic commission, "first for the Jew, then for the Gentile" (Romans 1:16); and we have reason to thank God that many Christian Hebrews are to be found in the ordinary membership and even the ministry of the churches of Christ.

Our Judea

But for us as individual Christians, what does this second stage of the Great Commission mean? Assuredly, that having begun at home, we are next to go with our testimony to our friends, to the whole circle of those we love and with whom we have personal influence and who belong to our sphere of fellowship and affection. Have we done so? Have you been true to your friends in witnessing for Christ? Have you, like Andrew and Philip, brought your brother and your friend to Jesus? Is your personal correspondence, your social conversation, your whole influence flavored and fragrant with the love of Christ and interwoven with tactful and wise appeals for the best and highest things; or has your selfishness, timidity and shame led you to betray your Master and neglect the very highest claims of holy friendship?

SECTION III—*Samaria*

The Gospel in Samaria

The Samaritans were a mongrel race descended from the old Jewish remnant left in Northern Palestine after the Assyrians took most of the people captive, and the heathen colonies with whom they intermarried after these immigrants were planted in the land by the Assyrian conquerors. Contrary to the laws and traditions of Israel, these poor Jews allowed themselves to be drawn into family relationships with the strangers, and thus there grew up a new hybrid race partly Jewish and partly heathen, with a mixture of Mosaic teaching and ritual along with much that was loose and uninspired. These people were called Samaritans, and as traitors to their race they were hated much worse than the heathen. The Jews, therefore, had no dealings with them; but the Lord during His own earthly ministry several times visited Samaria and opened the doors of salvation to these people. Now therefore, when giving the commission He was particular to include them, and at a very early date the Holy Spirit directed the first evangelists to go to them with the gospel. The pioneer of this work was Philip, the deacon. His work was marvelously successful, and in a short time a great revival ensued, multitudes flocking to Christ, so that the apostles and elders at Jerusalem were compelled to send a special deputation to visit these new churches and share with them the fuller blessings of the Holy Spirit. A little later we read of many churches in Samaria, as well as Judea, which were in a prosperous condition.

Our Samaria

Now what for us is the personal application of this third stage of apostolic witnessing? Where is our Samaria? Can we fail to recognize it in that great outlying world around us in the homeland, consisting of the multitudes that lie beyond the pale of Christian influences, whether it be by poverty or race distinctions or the awful effects and ravages of sin? They have grown up in every Christian land, a great multitude of outcast ones who never go to the house of God, whose synagogue is that of Satan, who worship the world, the flesh and the devil, who are held captive by Satan at his will, and for whom respectable Christianity remanded long ago to a place of hopeless despair. For the drunkard, the harlot, the thief, the convict, the foreign population who infest our alleys and slums, the multitudes that somehow struggle for life in the dark underworld of poverty and sin, it is only a little while since the very thought of salvation and rescue was seriously entertained among the activities of the Church of God. Thank God that it is coming to pass, and Christian love is now going out into the streets and lanes of the city to find the poor and the maimed, the halt and the blind. But oh, how much has yet to be done, and how little some of us have even attempted! Have you, beloved, been faithful there? This wonderful movement of rescue mission work in the homeland is one of the features of Christian life today and one of the signs of the end. The Holy Spirit is moving out and moving down from the old planes, and perhaps, leaving the gospel-hardened children of the kingdom and finding the chief trophies of grace today among these neglected and hopeless children of wretchedness and sin. When this task is fully done, and along with it the great outcast heathen world has been equally invited, then the Lord Himself will come.

SECTION IV—*The World*

The Gospel for the Heathen

"You will be my witnesses . . . to the ends of the earth" (Acts 1:8). This is the final stage and the supreme work of the witnessing Church. We shall find it the deep underlying thought of the whole book of Acts. It is quite wonderful and touching to see how the Lord patiently and gradually endeavored to bring His Church to understand this high calling and to be true to this trust. Naturally the Jew regarded the outlying Gentile world beyond the pale of God's purpose of grace. He believed he could not please God better than by keeping as far from them as possible, holding himself in a place of rigid separation and leaving them to their wickedness and doom. It was very difficult, therefore, to thoroughly infuse into the minds of the apostles themselves God's larger thought of love and salvation for the heathen. It is interesting to trace the unfolding of this purpose and plan through the book of Acts.

1. Pentecost

We notice in the gathering of the multitudes at Pentecost from all nations a providential movement in connection with the spread of the gospel. These people were brought from the remotest regions of the globe to attend the great annual Jewish festivals, and then God gave to them the marvelous lesson of Pentecost and sent them forth to tell the story in their own language and to their own people of this wonderful gospel. That in itself was a stupendous missionary movement and laid the foundation, no doubt, of many a church in far scattered lands.

2. Philip

Next we find Philip suddenly called from Samaria, in the midst of his work, to meet a heathen prince down in the desert of Gaza as he was returning disappointed and hungry-hearted to his distant home. Peter might have argued with Philip that there was work enough to do at home, for never were hands so full as his with that great revival in Samaria. But Philip left it all for the greater work of foreign missions, even as Judson and the early missionaries left the attractive fields of their own home churches, refusing the most flattering calls that they might go far hence unto the heathen. And Philip found his obedience was not misplaced. God never misfits. When the man is ready the field is ready, and lo, the gospel has been carried to Ethiopia, and the first convert of foreign missions has been sent forth as the pioneer of a nation and of a continent. Surely, it paid. And so no matter how busy or how needed you may seem to be at home, if God is calling you to the work of missions, do not hesitate, do not spare the best you have to give, do not fear to leave your work in other hands; enough that the "Lord has need of you."

3. Peter

Next, we have Peter's call to Caesarea and the house of Cornelius. First Peter himself had to be prepared, and there on the housetop God did most thoroughly prepare him, breaking up his old Jewish prejudices by that never-to-be-forgotten lesson of his strange, supernatural meal, and then calling him, when he had become enlarged enough to understand the call, to go to the capital of the country and the innermost circle of Roman influence and power and begin a new Pentecost in the very heart of the Roman Court. From that wonderful scene Peter went to Jerusalem with a testimony that they could not resist. "Who was I," he might well say, "to think that I could oppose God?" (11:17). And the apostles began to understand and to rejoice that the door of faith was at last open unto the Gentiles.

It was some such process as this that God had to go through in the beginning of this century in breaking our ecclesiastical fathers from their old theological shells and having them understand that it was our business to care for the heathen and send them the gospel. But, alas, even yet how little the ministry of the Church of God realizes the claims of foreign missions! We have no hesitation in saying that the lack of liberality, sacrifice and consecration in the churches of Christ lies much more at the door of the ministers than of the people themselves, and that when a pastor is thoroughly awakened to the claims of the perishing heathen and really baptized with the missionary spirit, there will never be any real difficulty in getting the people to give largely and to give freely. This is, perhaps, the most needed revival of missions in the Church of today.

4. Antioch

The next step in the development of the missionary idea was the church in Antioch. God had to have a new center from which to send out the great missionary movement. Jerusalem was too conservative and too exclusive, and so in Antioch a new center was started and a new mother church was formed—consisting of spirits like Barnabas, the noble merchant prince; Saul, the educated teacher; Manaen, the courtly gentleman; Simeon, the consecrated black man; Luke, the large-hearted cosmopolitan, and such men as these with a large mass of common people that had been brought into the church not even by apostolic preaching, but by the simple testimony of men and women like themselves. From this new center the gospel could go forth with peculiar power.

And so in our day God has been raising up His Antiochs again. The deep spiritual movements of our time all form a sort of Antioch from which are going forth the most vital missionary agencies of our time. It was this church that sent forth the early missionaries. Let us, therefore, not forget that it is God's plan to send forth the missionary from a warm home center. The idea of independent missions apart from that supporting center is not scriptural. There must be two ends to the work, the home and the foreign, both equally responsive and helping.

5. Barnabas and Saul, the First Missionaries

Time will only permit us to lightly touch this stirring theme. God has His men ready. Saul had been called from the ranks of the enemy, and Barnabas had also been prepared from another class. There were three men in the first missionary party. One was an educated teacher, and such men are needed still. The second was a consecrated businessman, and there are no better missionaries than such laymen. And there was a young man, a little fresh, a little immature, a little soft, a little weak, a little like some of our missionaries still—poor Mark. And he had his failure, as some of our boys and girls have at first, and for it Paul even would have none of him; but he came out all right at last. Let us learn the lesson of patience, for God even uses imperfect material and patiently waits until it is trained. And so they went forth, and in due time came back to tell the story of their wonderful beginning and to gather in that great missionary convention at Jerusalem, where the plan was more fully settled and their subsequent missionary work wrought out with still more intelligent and holy zeal. Let us learn the lessons of their victories and defeats, and let us catch the thought of the Master they followed so fully, so that He can use us to finish what they so gloriously began.

CHAPTER 4

WITNESSING FOR CHRIST

You will be my witnesses in Jerusalem, and in all Judea and Samaria, and to the ends of the earth. (Acts 1:8)

"I have appeared to you to appoint you as a servant and as a witness of what you have seen of me and what I will show you." . . . I have had God's help to this very day, and so I stand here and testify to small and great alike. (26:16, 22)

Testimony is the foundation of all jurisprudence in earthly courts and all faith in the economy of grace. The lives of men are determined every day by the word of a credible witness. And so God has rested the foundations of Christianity upon human testimony and required of us the faith that believes on the word of the true witness. God Himself meets us as a Witness.

Anyone who believes in the Son of God has this testimony in his heart. Anyone who does not believe God has made him out to be a liar, because he has not believed the testimony God has given about his Son. (1 John 5:10)

Faith is not believing because we have seen a mathematical demonstration, but it is believing someone's word. Therefore God has sent forth the most credible witnesses to bear testimony to men of the death and resurrection of Jesus Christ and the offer of salvation which He has made through His name. He has been most careful in the appointment of such witnesses. This was the primary meaning of the apostolic office to be witnesses of His resurrection (Acts 1:22). And for this purpose they were to be endued with supernatural power, that their testimony might be that of the Holy Spirit as well as of faithful men.

Our ministry, therefore, is that of witness-bearing. "You will be my witnesses in Jerusalem, and in all Judea and Samaria, and to the ends of the earth" (1:8).

Personal Knowledge

1. The witness must have personal knowledge of the matters concerning which he testifies. Hearsay evidence cannot be admitted. We must know Christ personally before we can testify to Him.

A personal experience is essential to effectiveness in all work for Christ. Men instinctively become sensible of the lack of it. It gives a fine tone and color to all we say, and its absence is quickly detected even by the unsaved. During the earlier years of the writer's ministry, before he knew the Holy Spirit personally, no one ever came to him to talk about the deeper life, but within 24 hours after he knew the Lord as an indwelling personal reality, hungry hearts began to come and ask the way to Jesus. You cannot deceive human souls with painted fire and spiritual illusions. We cannot make burning glasses for the heavenly altars out of lumps of ice as they do in Arctic regions to kindle fires.

> We must ourselves be true,
>   If we the truth would preach;
> Our hearts must overflow, if we
>   Another's heart would reach.

A Personal Christ

2. We are witnesses of a personal Christ. We are not sent to unfold a scheme of doctrine, a logical creed, a system of truth merely, but primarily, to tell about a Person, to make Jesus Christ real to men and make them long to know Him for themselves. We are not to testify of our personal experience so much as of Him; but we are to testify from our personal experience and have it give warmth, reality and force to the message of Jesus, as the heathen child so plaintively expressed it when she cried to the missionary, "Take me with you to your Jesus." We must have them feel that He is our Jesus, but it is Jesus and not ourselves that we are to preach. Your glowing experiences

may only perplex or discourage them and make them feel how unlike their experience is, or still worse, try to copy you. But let Christ be your theme, and you, like the transparent glass, reveal the light without projecting your own shadow.

Definite Testimony

3. Their witness of Jesus was at the same time very definite. It was not a vague metaphysical dream, such as Christian Science would give us, of some manifestation of Deity, some idea of love which God was projecting upon the human mind, but it was a real personal, individual Christ of whom they could tell with authority who He was, whence He came, how He suffered, died and rose again, where He is now and how He is coming once again.

Their testimony embraced four points especially.

First, they witnessed His divinity. He was "Jesus . . . the Son of God" (9:20). "The God of our fathers raised Jesus from the dead—whom you had killed by hanging him on a tree" (5:30). "God has made this Jesus, whom you crucified, both Lord and Christ" (2:36). That was the way they testified to Him.

Second, they saw His death and atonement. They witnessed to His sufferings and His precious blood as the ground of justification and forgiveness for sinful men.

Third, they witnessed of His resurrection. "God has raised this Jesus to life, and we are all witnesses of the fact" (2:32). They announced Him as a risen and glorified Being, seated on a throne of supreme power, and showing by the might of His very name that He was still alive and was the Son of God.

Fourth, their witness included His second coming. They preached Him to men as "judge of the living and the dead" (10:42). They proclaimed a day when God "will judge the world with justice by the man he has appointed. He has given proof of this to all men by raising him from the dead" (17:31). "He must remain in heaven until the time comes for God to restore everything, as he promised long ago through his holy prophets" (3:21). These were some of the terms in which they witnessed to His coming again. And so our witness of the Christ must always include His deity, His atonement, His resurrection and His coming again.

Scriptural Testimony

4. They testified according to the Scriptures, and they based their arguments on the Scriptures. In Peter's sermon in the second chapter of Acts we find him quoting with singular appropriateness from the prophet Joel and the patriarch David, arguments which they could not gainsay because they were from their own Scriptures. Again, in Acts 3:22 and 24, Moses and Samuel are called as witnesses to corroborate the apostolic testimony. So again we find Stephen basing his entire argument on the Old Testament history, and they

were powerless to resist the inexorable logic of his appeal. Philip in his interview with the eunuch, Acts 8:35, immediately turns to the Scriptures and from the book of Isaiah preaches unto him Jesus. Again in his great sermon at Antioch, Acts 13, Paul appeals to their own history as the foundation of his argument and quotes from David and the prophets (verses 33 and 41) to clinch his arguments and rivet his messages. So our testimony for Christ must be through His own Word, for the Bible is just one successive testimony of Jesus and every page a glowing portrait of His face.

In The Holy Spirit

5. Our witnessing must be in the power of the Spirit. "We are witnesses of these things," said Peter, "and so is the Holy Spirit, whom God has given to those who obey him" (5:32). It is the joint testimony of the Spirit and the messenger. Without Him our witness is cold and fruitless. "No one can say, 'Jesus is Lord,' except by the Holy Spirit" (1 Corinthians 12:3). And if we have the Holy Spirit the message cannot be kept back.

Official Witnesses

6. There were official witnesses and unofficial. There were the appointed messengers and officers of the church, and there were the hearts and voices that overran the limits of conventional ministry and just witnessed because they could not help it, going beyond their own province, but gloriously irregular through the power of the Spirit.

First there was the apostolic body, consisting only of those who had seen the Lord in the flesh and were qualified thus to be witnesses of His resurrection. Therefore there can be no apostolic succession, for John saw on the foundations of the New Jerusalem the names, not of all the apostles of later times, but the 12 apostles of the Lamb.

Then there were the prophets, whose ministry Paul defines thus: "Everyone who prophesies speaks to men for their strengthening, encouragement and comfort" (1 Corinthians 14:3). The prophet, therefore, is a God-touched messenger who brings to men some living message of instruction or appeal or consolation fresh from the heart of God. He is not necessarily the foreteller of future events. Certainly he is not inspired to give a new Bible or authoritative revelations of the will of God in addition to the Holy Scriptures, but he is just a voice to speak from time to time in living power what God has already spoken through His written Word.

Then the evangelist came next, the soul winner, the messenger of salvation to men, with a wider parish than a single church, an office which still God uses and honors, and should be recognized as the special ministry of those whom the Holy Spirit thus calls.

Next was the office of pastor and teacher. He was the shepherd of the particular congregation, and associated with him was the elder, an office that included two classes apparently, the teaching and the ruling elder, for the apostle speaks of elders that labor both in word and doctrine as worthy of double honor.

The deacon was the servant of the church as the word literally means. His duty was to minister to the poor, the stranger, the neglected, to stand with open heart and hand at the threshold of the church, bidding its children welcome to the Father's house and helping to make it indeed a household of faith and a home of love.

The deaconess, too, had her place, for Phoebe, "a servant of the church in Cenchrea" (Romans 16:1), was literally a deaconess as the words mean.

Then there were the irregulars of the Lord's army, the people that went beyond their formal line of ministry, and like Joseph, allowed their fruit to "climb over a wall" (Genesis 49:22). Such was Stephen, the deacon, who became the most illustrious evangelist and the first martyr of the infant Church, confounding even Saul in the synagogues of the Cilicians with his matchless arguments and heavenly wisdom, and bringing him by his dying prayers to follow in the same pathway. Such was Philip, also a deacon, who through his zeal and faith promoted to be the great evangelist of Samaria and afterward pioneer missionary of Africa, calling the prince of Ethiopia to Christ and sending him back to his own land, perhaps, to lay the foundations of the great churches which we afterward find in those regions.

And then woman's ministry, too, found its place; good Priscilla getting ahead even of her husband Aquila in the ranks of service, and Dorcas with her spirit-baptized fingers and heart strings so necessary to the apostolic Church that she had to be brought back even from the dead, while James the apostle was permitted to pass away in martyrdom. Such were the apostolic witnesses in whose footsteps we are permitted to follow in the closing days of the same dispensation. There was a glorious irregularity as well as a divine order, for order was never intended to cramp, but only to direct the forces of the spiritual world. Therefore we find in Acts 8:4, that when persecution came all the Christians were scattered abroad except the apostles, and "those who had been scattered preached the word wherever they went." This word "preached" is an unusual word, meaning literally, talking informally, or as some have translated it, "gossiping the gospel." It was the witness-bearing of plain men and women who just talked about Jesus wherever they went, and so talked that, as we read a little later in Acts 11:19–21, they brought a great multitude to Christ and laid the foundations of the mother church at Antioch, which became henceforth the head and heart of the missionary activities of the apostolic Church.

Examples

7. Here are some examples of their witness-bearing:

Peter on the Day of Pentecost

a. We have Peter's testimony on the day of Pentecost, which Professor Stiffler characterizes as the most compact and convincing piece of sacred oratory in the New Testament. And yet it was an address that could be delivered in less than 10 minutes, and had none of the shallow tricks of modern oratory about it, but was the simple eloquence of truth and earnestness on fire with the Holy Spirit.

Peter before the Council

b. Next were Peter's messages before the Council, splendid examples of a holy courage that cared not for his own safety, but sought only to make the occasion an opportunity to witness for his Savior and Master. And so convincing was the testimony that the rulers were compelled to let him alone and keep their hands off the word of God.

Stephen's Testimony

c. Again we have the testimony of Stephen, so bold and fearless of his own safety, so wise and convincing in its arguments, and so heavenly in its spirit, that the only argument left them in their baffled rage was a shower of stones, making him, as the word witness literally means, a martyr too, the proto-martyr of the Church of God.

Philip's Witness

d. Then we have the witness of Philip in Samaria, and later to the eunuch in the desert, and in both instances it was the same simple testimony: "Philip went down to a city in Samaria and proclaimed the Christ there" (8:5). "Then Philip began with that very passage of Scripture and told him the good news about Jesus" (8:35)—the same old gospel whether in Samaria or Africa:

Jesus only, Jesus ever,
    Jesus all our theme shall be.

Peter's Testimony

e. Next we have the witness of Peter in the house of Cornelius, a beautiful model of gospel preaching. It took a good deal to get him ready for it. God had to take him on the housetop and put him through some pretty hard classes, not only in theology, but also in biology, before he was ready to go to a Gentile congregation and preach Jesus unto them. But he was ready at last, and preach he did, so that the Holy Spirit came like a second Pentecost, and the door of faith was opened unto the Gentiles. What a sermon that was in Acts 10:34-43, only 200 words all told, less than five minutes long and yet the whole gospel compressed into it without the slightest stiffness: all about John's baptism, Jesus Christ's life on earth, His death on the cross, His resurrection and its infallible proofs, His coming again as the Judge of the quick and the dead and His offer of salvation to all that believe witnessed by all the prophets. Nothing lacking. Everything complete and glowing with the very love of Christ.

Paul the Witness

f. Next we have Paul's witness-bearing. It began

immediately after his conversion. "At once he began to preach in the synagogues that Jesus is the Son of God" (9:20). Time will not permit us to follow all the recorded testimonies of his life and work: at Antioch, Acts 13, a scriptural testimony to the Jews; at Derbe and Lystra, Acts 14, an entirely different but equally appropriate testimony to a heathen audience; at Athens, Acts 17, a still more wonderful and wisely adapted appeal to the extraordinary audience gathered at the Acropolis at Athens representing all the art, learning and idolatry of Greece, but all woven into the exquisite web of his testimony of Jesus, the coming Judge of all, and the risen Son of God—a message followed even in cold Athens by the conversion of a poor prostitute and a noble councilor. Then we might trace also with equal interest his witness to the jailer of Philippi: "Believe in the Lord Jesus, and you will be saved" (16:31); his strenuous testimony at Corinth (18:5); and the long retrospect he gives us in Acts 20 of his three years' ministry and his faithful witness-bearing at Ephesus until he could say, "I am innocent of the blood of all men" (20:26). Again we have his testimony from the stairs of the castle in Jerusalem (chapter 22), addressed to his own countrymen; his heart-searching message to Felix and Drusilla (chapters 24, 25), until the old Roman debauchee trembled on his very throne and for a moment felt himself in the presence of the judgment day; and his longest testimony with the story of his conversion as told by himself in the presence of Agrippa in the 26th chapter of Acts—all these messages are brimming with the glory and the name of Jesus Christ, and his one object is not to clear himself, but to introduce his Master. Later on we see him on the deck of the tossing vessel in the Adriatic storm, taking command of the ship when all hearts failed with terror, and testifying of Jesus Christ, "whose I am and whom I serve" (27:23), until he himself becomes the central figure in the drama, and for his sake all on board are saved. At Rome it is the same story. Daily in his own hired house they come to him, and the book of Acts leaves him there preaching the kingdom of God and teaching those things which concerned the Lord Jesus Christ with all confidence, no man forbidding him, for two long years. His later epistles give us innumerable glimpses of subsequent testimonies.

In the closing scenes unveiled in his last letter to Timothy, we see him brought before the cruel Nero on trial for his life. We hear him say with no bitterness of spirit, only sorrow for them,

> At my first defense, no one came to my support, but everyone deserted me. May it not be held against them. But the Lord stood at my side and gave me strength, so that through me the message might be fully proclaimed and all the Gentiles might hear it. And I was delivered from the lion's mouth. (2 Timothy 4:16–17)

We can almost hear the growls of the fierce Nubian lions that were appointed for his death. We can see the great crowd of Gentiles gathered round the court of Nero waiting for the verdict, and whether their thumbs shall be turned upward for his acquittal or downward for his doom. But what do we see on the part of Paul? No thought of danger, no fear of death, no notice of the angry lion, but only one purpose, that "the message might be fully proclaimed" (4:17). It is the chance of his life. For the first and last time he has the ear of Nero, and the old sinner shall hear the gospel now if he never did before. And Paul just preaches it with all his might until not only he, but all the Gentiles, hear once at least the story of Jesus Christ. That was his business. What about the lion? That was God's business. And in the most incidental manner he just adds, "I was delivered from the lion's mouth. The Lord will rescue me from every evil attack and will bring me safely to his heavenly kingdom. To him be glory for ever and ever. Amen" (4:17–18). It was his business to take care of Christ's glory, and it was Christ's business to take care of him.

LESSONS

In conclusion:

1. Have something to tell and something to give, and it will get out like the testimony of which Peter had to say, "We cannot help speaking about what we have seen and heard" (Acts 4:20).

2. Always hold up Jesus Christ and try to make

Him real to the world. That is the only thing that will attract, that will save, that will satisfy, that will help lost men and bring God's blessing.

3. Begin at home. That is your Jerusalem. Then go to every widening circle of influence and opportunity until you reach the uttermost part of the earth.

4. Recognize every situation that comes to you as an opportunity for testimony. Look at every person you meet as a subject for God's blessing through you in some way, and thus all your life will be a ministry for Him.

5. Live your testimony, be a Bible. If you cannot be an apostle you can be a "letter . . . known and read by everybody" (2 Corinthians 3:2).

6. Ask God to put into your life supernatural things that will themselves be His witness to your testimony and commend it to an unbelieving world. Every Christian ought to have answered prayers in his body, in his business, in his trials and temporal circumstances, that will speak for God and make them know that there is a real and a living Christ, and that our Christianity is not a theory but is supernatural and divine.

7. Remember that though you may never be a missionary in Africa or China, you can still be a witness to the uttermost part of the earth. You can shine afar through other lives even where your feet may never go. At a country crossing and beside a village pump, Brainerd Taylor met a young man and spoke to him a few simple, burning words that sent him to seek and find the Lord, and

at length become a missionary to the heathen. He never knew the name of his benefactor until long years had passed and Brainerd Taylor had been a good while in heaven. Then one day there fell into his hands a little book containing the story of that saintly life and the portrait of the man on the frontispiece. Then for the first time he knew to whom it was he owed his salvation and his life's work, and falling upon his knees he thanked God for the saintly man who had never been able himself to go to Africa, but whose witness was being repeated through another life in that dark land. God give us grace to receive our Pentecost and fulfill our testimony.

CHAPTER 5

TO THE REGIONS BEYOND

Some time later Paul said to Barnabas, "Let us go back and visit the brothers in all the towns where we preached the word of the Lord and see how they are doing." (Acts 15:36)

Paul and his companions traveled throughout the region of Phrygia and Galatia, having been kept by the Holy Spirit from preaching the word in the province of Asia. When they came to the border of Mysia, they tried to enter Bithynia, but the Spirit of Jesus would not allow them to. So they passed by Mysia and went down to Troas. During the night Paul had a vision of a man of Macedonia standing and begging him, "Come over to Macedonia and help us." (16:6–9)

In a previous chapter we have reviewed the plan of the Holy Spirit and the apostolic Church for the wider witnessing of the gospel from Jerusalem to the uttermost part of the earth, and we have

seen how God's supreme thought for the evangelization of the world was slowly impressed upon
the early Church until the great work of foreign
missions had been fairly started with the first missionary journey of Barnabas and Paul. All this
was, indeed, a marked advance on Jewish conservatism, and forcibly recalls the slow awakening of
the modern Church during the past century to a
sense of its obligations to the heathen world.

But it was merely a beginning. They were as
yet but feeling their way to this new department
of work and finding out its limitations and spiritual laws. At the end of their journey it was necessary that the Church should come together and
have a more perfect understanding of God's great
plan for the evangelization of a world, so that they
might go forth and work intelligently in coopera-
tion with their divine Leader.

The Council at Jerusalem

For this purpose the first Council at Jerusalem
was held, to which we referred in the close of
the last chapter. The effect of this was to clearly
determine in the minds of both Jewish and Gentile Christians the divine method for the present
age, namely, the gathering out from the Gentiles
a people for His name; second, the personal
coming of the Lord Jesus immediately afterward; third, the millennial age and the salvation
of all the world. With all this settled and com-
municated in the form of a fraternal letter to the
brethren in all the churches, they were now

ready to enter fully upon the great business of the world's evangelization, and the present section beginning with the second great missionary journey marks the next epoch in this mighty movement.

Revisiting Their Stations

It began with the revisitation of the stations already planted, and then followed the evangelization of the Celtic tribes of the highlands of Asia, known as the Galatians. But at this point God called a halt in all their home work in the continent of Asia, and marked a new epoch by sending them forth to the yet unoccupied continent of Europe, in connection with which the rest of their campaign was entirely occupied.

Let us make a passing note of time at this point, that we may the more intelligently follow this great historical movement. It was now about 17 years since Pentecost. The events of the last section, from the sending out of the first missionaries to the Council at Jerusalem, had occupied about three or four years; and the present section, embracing their work in Galatia and Greece to the close of their second missionary journey, covered about three years more, from A.D. 51 to 54. While the narrative sweeps rapidly over these stirring events, let us not forget that what we are told is but a fragment of the whole story of apostolic missions, and that these are but sample pages from God's book of remembrance intended to give a connected thread of the development of missions, especially in connection with the life and work of the great apostle of missions, Paul.

Second Missionary Journey

Let us mark some of the stages of this second missionary campaign (Acts 16 to 18):

1. Voluntary

We note the absence of the special call of God to go forth as in their first missionary journey. It was voluntary, and came directly from the prompting of Paul himself. "Let us go back," he said to Barnabas, "and visit the brothers" (15:36). And so we learn that when God has once called us to His work we are to be about our Father's business and not wait for some special revelation for each new ministry, but "each man, as responsible to God, should remain in the situation God called him to" (1 Corinthians 7:24).

2. Timothy

We note in the next place the solicitude of Paul about his fellow workers. He wanted the best material only for this great work, and he would have nothing to do with Mark, who had proved a failure in their former journey and gone back from Perga when the difficulties began to thicken. We can scarcely doubt that Paul was right in wanting the best missionaries, and we are quite safe in following his example. We cannot doubt that Barnabas was right, too, in standing by Mark as his nephew and helping to restore him to the Lord and the work, and so successful was he that the outcome justified him, and the day came when Paul was manly enough to acknowledge Mark's merits and even to send for him in the hour of his need and add, "he is helpful to me in my ministry" (2 Timothy 4:11). Doubtless Paul's firmness was as much used as Barnabas' kindness in restoring the young and yet undisciplined lad.

But the best lesson of all is the beautiful picture we have here of the way in which love can settle the differences of consecrated Christians. There are two ways of separating from our fellow workers: one, which leaves an unhealed scar, and weakens both of our lives for all the future; the other, like the separation of Abraham and Lot, or Barnabas and Paul, which sheds honor on the character of both and starts two centers instead of one of holy influence and service. If you cannot work together in perfect harmony as Christians, separate in perfect frankness and Christian love.

3. Silas

We soon find God supplying Paul with new companions as he sets out on his missionary journey, leaving Barnabas to divide the field and go back to Cyprus, his native island, while Paul takes his own home province of Cilicia and moves on to Asia Minor. Paul chooses Silas as his fellow worker, and a little later God gives him Timothy who had been converted three years before during the apostle's former visit to

Derbe and Lystra. Timothy was the son of a godly mother, Eunice, a Jewess, and indeed had enjoyed the blessed teaching of a godly grandmother, Lois. There is, perhaps, a hereditary piety; at least there is an early influence in the first teaching and training of childhood that nothing can be a substitute for. God have mercy on the children of worldly, shallow, heartless mothers, and have mercy on mothers who bring into being neglected lives to a fate worse than orphanage. We little dream how soon the infant mind begins to receive religious impressions. I know a little child, little more than three years old, who can tell the whole story of the Acts of the Apostles, and often goes aside with her Christian nurse at her own request, with the tears streaming down her little face, to pray for the conversion of the manservant in the house to whom she is much attached, but who, she has lately found, is going to dancing school, and she greatly fears he will lose his soul. In Timothy's case the soil was all prepared, and he needed only the seed of the gospel and the quickening of the Spirit to bring into birth the most beautiful Christian life of the apostolic story, except, perhaps, the apostle Paul himself. From the first he became like a very child to his spiritual father.

> I have no one else like him, who takes a genuine interest in your welfare. For everyone looks out for his own interests, not those of Jesus Christ. But you know that Timothy

has proved himself, because as a son with his father he has served with me in the work of the gospel. (Philippians 2:20–22)

Timothy was the son of a Gentile father and a Jewish mother, and in order to smooth down the prejudices of the Jews, Paul on this occasion consented to his being circumcised, and so Timothy became a sort of bridge between the two classes who were united among Paul's hearers.

4. Former Fields Revisited

The revisiting of the churches already planted was first carefully attended to. There seem to have been many of these, and it is added, "So the churches were strengthened in the faith and grew daily in numbers" (Acts 16:5). The nurturing of that little flock was quite as important a missionary work as the planting of the gospel in new fields. In our zeal for evangelization we must never lose sight of edification, the building up of the body of Christ. The Lord Jesus has covered both in the Great Commission, "Go and make disciples of all nations, baptizing them in the name of the Father and of the Son and of the Holy Spirit" (Matthew 28:19). That is the work of planting the gospel. But we must never forget the other work which follows: "teaching them to obey everything I have commanded you" (28:20).

5. Galatia

One new church, at least, was planted during

this journey. Luke passes over it in the narrative with a single word, but the epistle to the Galatians tells the story of its planting. It was among the highlanders of Asia, the Celtic ancestors of the French, the Irish and the Gaelic people of the north of Scotland. Like their descendants still, they were a fiery, passionate race, full of enthusiasm for a new doctrine and as ready to follow some brilliant, false teacher into error. Therefore Paul tells us, "You welcomed me as if I were an angel of God" (Galatians 4:14), but a little later we find them going away after Judaizing teachers into ritualism. To them we owe one of the richest of the Pauline epistles. But with this new station their work in Asia came to a close.

6. A Halt

The time had now come for a new departure even in foreign missions. The old world which for 4,000 years had been the cradle of the race, and the seat of all its religious movements, must now give place to the new continent of Europe and its children, which were to fill a larger place in the history of the future than even Asia had in the past. And so a strange incident occurs. They find their evangelistic work apparently arrested, "having been kept by the Holy Spirit from preaching the word in the province of Asia" (Acts 16:6), whither they were pressing forward to the ancient city of Ephesus. "When they came to the border of Mysia, they tried to enter Bithynia, but the Spirit of Jesus would not allow them to" (16:7). It must have seemed strange at first and hard to understand. They had been so accustomed to the presence and blessing of the Spirit in all their meetings that they may have been tempted to think there was something wrong in them. And so, perhaps, for several weeks they persevered and tried to push forward into these new fields. But everywhere it was the same. God would not go with them. They were evidently out of His order and will. And so, like wise men, they stopped and waited.

Have you never found at some point in your Christian work that God seemed to call a halt, and that the blessing that you had enjoyed appeared to desert you and the work to grow heavy and fruitless? And yet you could find nothing in your own heart to condemn. After a while, perhaps, it dawned upon you that God did not want you there, but had some other calling which He was trying to show you. Is this perhaps the reason why so much of our Christian work at home is dead, and worse than dead—corrupt? And why our theological seminaries and pulpits are teaching higher criticism, and our church members are dancing down in the great whirl of worldliness and sin to apostasy and ruin? God is not blessing His Church, because she is not where He wants her. She is wasting her energy, her money, her ministry, in religious selfishness, ecclesiastical extravagance and ritualistic forms in the name of religion, while her people are spending their God-given prosperity in every form of indulgence and selfishness. If she would only call a halt like Paul and Timothy and wait before the Lord as they did, the light would soon come, and she would find that her blessings are cursed because she is spending them on herself and neglecting the perishing world.

7. Europe

While they wait at Troas the situation immediately becomes plain. God does not want them any longer in Asia because He needs them more in Europe. And so there appears to Paul a vision by night, a man of Macedonia beckoning and crying, "Come over to Macedonia and help us" (16:9). And when the morning dawns the little company confer together and immediately conclude God is calling them to Macedonia. Taking passage at the earliest moment they sail for Philippi, the chief city of a miniature Roman state. Finding work, no doubt, as skilled laborers, they spend the week quietly, and on the Sabbath day they search in vain for the usual synagogue of Jewish worshipers. But they learn that there is a little company of pious Jews accustomed to meet outside the town by the riverside, and thither they find their way.

And so the gospel in the great continent of Europe begins with a woman's prayer meeting, and indeed with the opening of a woman's heart, for "The Lord opened her heart to respond to Paul's message" (16:14). Why not? Hers has ever been the glory of undoing the shame of the fall. The conversion of Lydia opened the doors of her home, and the little church was immediately transferred to that loving household. It is not strange that henceforth the spirit of the Philippian church and Paul's relation to it were marked by a tenderness not found in any other case.

8. *Opposition at Philippi*

Soon, however, the dark shadow of the adversary falls upon the scene. Satan understands the situation and tries to meet it in its worst form. A priestess of Apollo, inflated with demoniac possession, and yet constrained somehow to bear testimony to the divine character of the missionaries, pursues them from day to day with her insane ravings, and at the same time with her witness to them and to their message, until they are constrained to meet the issue. Then Paul, in the name of Jesus Christ, demands the demon to depart and sets her free from Satan's power. But this, of course, immediately stops her profession and brings upon the disciples the anger of her employers, who used her clairvoyant gift for purposes of gain. A riot ensues, and by a skillful appeal to the prejudices of the multitude on the ground that they are subverting Roman customs, they are condemned. They are cruelly beaten, bound with stocks and chains and cast into the inner prison. It seems, indeed, as if Satan has triumphed.

9. *The Victory*

It is never defeat so long as we do not lose our song of praise, and that was something the Philippian dungeon could not take away from these early missionaries. They prayed in their dismal dungeon until they could pray no more, for prayer had changed to praise, and they sang their gladness and their triumph until the strange sounds echoed through the dreary corridors and woke up the wondering prisoners. But soon the answer came from the heavenly listeners. There was a great earthquake, but such an earthquake was never known before. Instead of destroying the prison and crushing the inmates to death, it acted with the strangest intelligence, only slipping back the prison bolts and shaking off the fetters from the apostles and the prisoners. That was indeed a grand encore to their song of praise. No wonder the jailer was terrified. No wonder next morning the officials were alarmed. There was something more than a political complication in the situation. The hand of God was here. The victory of faith had been followed by the victory of Almighty power, and best of all, of saving grace, for the brutal jailer who had so needlessly aggravated the torture of his prisoners, casting them into the inner prison and making their feet fast in stocks, was now pleading for mercy, and a little later rejoicing in his new-found Savior and entertaining his prisoners with his converted household in his own home. Next morning witnessed a still more marked triumph. The very authorities, learning that they had beaten a freeborn Roman and thus insulted the majesty of the empire, sent the pleading message to Paul and his companions to please get out of prison as quietly as possible and say nothing about it. But Paul was a man as well as a missionary, and he stood upon his dignity for Christ's sake and for the sake of the little flock he represented, as the true Christian ever should. Nothing less than an honorable discharge would he accept, and so God vindicated him before the whole community and the highest authorities of the city. But now his victory being complete, it is fitting that he should show a triumph of another kind in the spirit of meekness, which is even higher than the spirit of manhood. His work in Philippi is done, and he determines quietly to retire without pressing his advantage or humiliating his enemies, and so he quietly takes his leave of the beloved little flock, and passing on along the old Roman road 100 miles westward, he pauses next at Thessalonica.

10. Thessalonica

We cannot linger over the triumphs of the gospel in Thessalonica and Berea, marked as they were by the usual introduction through the Jewish synagogue, the first fruits that always followed in Jewish and Gentile converts, and then the bitter persecution of the angry Jews from which the apostle withdrew when his pioneer work was done and hastened on to new fields.

11. Athens

We must linger over that dramatic scene on the Acropolis of Athens, where Christianity came face to face with the cultured heathenism of Greece and the world. If there be an atmosphere more difficult than any other to penetrate with the message of the gospel, it is that of intellectual and fashionable frivolity. Luke aptly describes Athenian society by a phrase that might not unfittingly be applied to many of our modern social circles. "All the Athenians and the foreigners who lived there spent their time doing nothing but talking about and listening to the latest ideas" (17:21).

Against this frivolous spirit the gospel strikes as a cannonball upon a wall of sandbags. If it was solid rock it might be battered down, but the soft sand just falls over it and fills the vacuum, like the waves after the keel of the passing ship, leaving no impression behind. No wonder that such congregations break the hearts of earnest ministers and wear out even the long-suffering of God. Such an audience now confronted the great apostle. Little cared he for the sights of Athens. "He was greatly distressed to see that the city was full of idols" (17:16). At length the opportunity came, and the message was equal to the occasion. It deserves to be written in letters of gold.

First it began with inimitable tact; complimenting his religious audience, he politely reminded them that he perceived that they were "very religious" (17:22). Then he told them the happy incident of the altar that he had just discovered to an unknown god whom they were endeavoring to worship, and about whom they must wish to know. He had come to tell them all about Him.

And then began that marvelous setting of Christianity over against Greek philosophy and mythology. Standing in the midst of an audience that had no faith in God, he began by pronouncing that one name, "God," with an emphasis that must have rung in thundering accents from all the splendid array of sculpture and architecture around. Addressing a people that were materialists and denied the doctrine of creation, he next added, "God who made the world and everything in it" (17:24). Looking in the face of a crowd of pantheists, who identified matter with God, he declared, "God . . . is the Lord of heaven and earth and does not live in temples built by hands" (17:24). Addressing an audience of exclusive Greeks who looked upon the rest of the world as barbarians, he dared to tell them, "From one man he made every nation of men" (17:26). Surveying a whole forest of sculptured statues of innumerable gods and goddesses, he reminded them that "we should not think that the divine being is like gold or silver or stone—an image made by man's design and skill" (17:29). Then growing more deeply solemn, he told them that "in the past God overlooked such ignorance, but now he commands all people everywhere to repent" (17:30), and soon would meet them in the great judgment day, face to face with that Man of whom He witnessed, "He has given proof of this to all men by raising him from the dead" (17:31).

The whole address could be repeated in five or six minutes, and yet it outweighs whole volumes of philosophy, theology and diluted homiletics. It was cut short by ironical sneers and a mocking and polite request to defer the remainder of his address to some other occasion. But out of this five minute address came the conversion of one of the distinguished council of the Areopagus, and Damaris, who seems to have been a woman of the town, with others not named. Even in cold, heartless Athens, God's Word could not return to Him void.

12. Corinth

Our space will only permit us to touch for a moment the closing scene of this great missionary journey. Forty-five miles south, and almost visible from the heights of Mars Hill, was the rich commercial city of Corinth. It was the maritime capital of the western world and the metropolis of its vice and sin. Here for a year and a half Paul continued to labor, until he had closed his successful ministry in Greece and the gospel was firmly established in the continent of Europe. The story of Corinth was a record of faith, trial and marvelous victory.

Conclusion

The whole section emphasizes again and again that great missionary plan which God had so clearly projected upon their vision at the commencement. The keynote of every incident was "to the ends of the earth" (1:8). The watchword of every step was "farther on." The heart of God was reaching out with intense solicitude to the unevangelized, and it is needless to say that still that heart is as intensely concerned for the "regions beyond" (2 Corinthians 10:16). Along with this we constantly hear the echo of that other message, "from the Gentiles a people for himself" (Acts 15:14). It is not an evangelistic movement to convert the world, but to gather out of the world an elect people for His coming. We find this again at Antioch, where "all who were appointed for eternal life believed" (13:48); and we find it in the last scene at Corinth, where the Master's message to His apostle is, "I have many people in this city" (18:10). Corinth is not to be converted, Greece is not to be a Christian nation, but God has people there whom He must find.

And finally, the supreme lesson that accompanies us all the way is that the work is God's and the power must be God's alone. It was not Paul that converted Lydia, but the Lord opened Lydia's heart. Your camera may be all right, your lens may be perfect, your focus may be exact, your film may be chemically prepared and everything ready for the picture, but without yonder sun there will be no impression on that film. It is the sun that makes the photograph, not the artist. And so the work of the Acts of the Apostles, the work of the Church of God to the end of time, the work of every minister and every missionary, the conversion and sanctification of every soul is God's and God's alone, to whom be glory forever and ever. Amen.

CHAPTER 6

A CHAPTER FROM ONE OF PAUL'S MISSIONARY JOURNEYS

One night the Lord spoke to Paul in a vision: "Do not be afraid; keep on speaking, do not be silent." (Acts 18:9)

Finally, brothers, pray for us that the message of the Lord may spread rapidly and be honored, just as it was with you. And pray that we may be delivered from wicked and evil men, for not everyone has faith. But the Lord is faithful, and he will strengthen and protect you from the evil one. (2 Thessalonians 3:1–3)

We have been sweeping with rapid flight over Paul's great missionary journeys. Today we shall tarry for a while with him at one of his stations, and see the closing of his second great missionary journey in the city of Corinth. It is full of incidents fraught with instruction and inspiration to every Christian heart and missionary worker.

His Coming to Corinth

We saw him last at Athens, in a city cold and utterly heartless. He must have been glad to leave its cheerless atmosphere. He had probably seen from Athens, 45 miles to the south, a sharp cliff rising off the horizon, and perhaps he may have discerned the town nestling at its feet. Certainly he would have seen the beautiful harbors on either side and the countless ships docked there.

Down this well-traveled highway he took his way to Corinth probably on foot, for we find him on other occasions walking many long miles. He went alone, for he had sent Timothy and Silas from Athens to Thessalonica to cheer the brethren there, for they needed them more. Paul was a bighearted friend and loved congenial company. His solitude, therefore, was due to his unselfishness.

On his approaching Corinth the first thing he would have seen was the citadel known as the Acrocorinthus. It was a splendid crag rising 2,000 feet, a sheer cliff against the sky, and stood above the city of Corinth. The city was built at its foot, and at the top was a little city and powerful fortress. As he drew nearer he reached the narrow isthmus which joins the peninsula to the mainland of Greece.

On each side was a splendid harbor—one the emporium of all the commerce of the East, the other reaching out to the western Mediterranean. These two harbors were crowded with the commerce of the world, and Corinth was the commercial metropolis of the earth. It was filled with Jews, Greeks and Italians. It was a place of immense wealth and vast trade; also, alas, of great wickedness, where all colors and classes of men constantly came together. So wicked was it that the word "Corinthian" has come down to our own day to describe the worst class of women.

This was the city to which Paul was now coming, but with all its wickedness, it was a great relief to get out of cold, heartless Athens. It is easier to preach the gospel in Wall Street or the Bowery than in the chilling atmosphere of Fifth Avenue fashion.

Paul was wise in choosing the great centers of life for his headquarters in mission work. The cities of the world control its life. And so God would have us as we go to preach the gospel, to work from the center to the circumference.

Aquila and Priscilla

What were his business and domestic arrangements when he came to his mission field? He did not have a big society behind him to send him large drafts each month, and it is not likely he had very many coins in his wallet. But he had a skilled and strong right hand. He knew how to weave hair cloth and put a tent together. When he reached Corinth he began to "look for a job," as we would say. He soon found it in the factory or shop of two good people, Aquila and Priscilla, Jews, his own countrymen, who had been expelled from Rome through a decree of Claudius Caesar.

The incident is given in profane history. Claudius Caesar had become so disgusted with the quarrels of the Jews about One named Christos or Christ, that he turned all the Jews out. Aquila and Priscilla went to the provinces to find a resting place. It is quite evident that at this time Aquila and Priscilla were not Christians. If so, we would have been told that Paul went to them because they were believers. Instead we are simply told they were of the same craft. They met in the workshop and then they invited him to their home, and he went with them. This was the beginning of that splendid stream of holy helpfulness that filled so large a place in ancient Christianity and in the story of Paul himself.

There are two things well worthy of our notice right here: first, the honest, manly independence of the missionary. He did not carry his hat in his hand asking people to give him help, but worked for his needs and the needs of them that were with him. And he could do this and trust God, too. It is all right to trust God as well as your own right hand. The people that work can best trust. The businessman has just as good a chance to live the faith life as the man that has no business. Manhood is always at a premium in personal influence and Christian work. So Paul was always independent. Speaking from this very place a little later to the Thessalonians to whom he wrote, he speaks of his honest industry and tells them how "we worked night and day in order not to be a burden to anyone while we preached the gospel of God to you" (1 Thessalonians 2:9).

Then again what a beautiful picture he gives of their fellowship in their daily calling. It was the beginning of a lifelong fellowship in higher things. What are you doing for the man that works alongside of you? And what about that woman that comes to help you in your household with her manual toil? Think about this, dear men and women, for most of us are called of God to the most honorable of all callings, that of honest independent labor, and in these days of restless speculation we cannot too much emphasize the honor and importance of honest labor and simple independence as honest working men and examples to our fellow men. May the day never come when labor will be discounted! Paul's father, though he must have been rich, and certainly gave Paul a good education, taught him a trade, and every true father and mother should teach their children some trade or occupation by which they may be independent.

Still another question comes up—what about the people that live with you, and the people with whom you live? Aquila and Priscilla took Paul home; they were true home missionaries. That is where the greatest of all preachers begins, the mother, and where our influence tells more intimately, more continuously and more eternally than anywhere else. Beloved, is your family circle, where they live with you, a place where your life is speaking for God, even as the story of Paul and

Aquila and Priscilla? Their friendship is one of the most blessed pictures in the whole story of Acts. Here we have the beginning of it. They were thrown together in the same family circle, and Paul's influence over them led them to Christ, and their influence with Apollos and others made them his helpers in the gospel.

A Sabbath at Corinth—His Public Ministry

Now the Sabbath has come. There is a synagogue there. On the Sabbath day they are gathered in it, and Paul, of course, finds his way there. He keeps the Sabbath. No man ought to be so busy that he loses God's day of rest—the day that God wants not so much for Himself as for the good of man. You will never lose anything by taking care of God's holy day.

Next we find him in the synagogue, in his place in the congregation. He began at doors that God had opened and he did not turn his back upon the Jews and the synagogue until they turned him out. That is the place for us to begin, and if they turn us out God will open other doors. We are told very simply that he went to the synagogue and reasoned with them on the Sabbath, and persuaded the Jews and the Greeks. Those two words "reasoned" and "persuaded" give us the whole gist of Paul's splendid ministry. He gave them facts, foundations, the truth; he appealed to their understanding, he took the Scripture and opened it up to them. But it was no cold logic nor all logic. When he was through reasoning, he began to persuade them. Oh, how the tears would get into his voice and the fire would burn in his tones! The first appealed to the intellect, and the second appealed to the conscience, the heart and the will.

So he began his ministry, and for a time there seemed to be little result. But now something happens.

Reinforcements—Silas and Timothy

We come to the next act in the drama, and we find a new inspiration coming to our missionary. "When Silas and Timothy came from Macedonia, Paul devoted himself exclusively to preaching, testifying to the Jews that Jesus was the Christ" (Acts 18:5). Something happened; two dear hearts had arrived. It was the touch of the hand of a friend, and thank God for the touch of the hand of a friend! How it cheers the heart of the lone worker on the field when he sees the new missionary coming! It is like fresh waters to a thirsty soul to have news from a far country. Let us think of our lone workers and help to cheer them by sending reinforcements. Now Paul could preach. He got up the next day and they wondered what was the matter with him as his face glowed and his voice rose into notes of passion, and he pleaded and warned and wept until they thought something must have happened. Do you help people that way? Does your coming to them make any difference in their work? Have you a bright face and a warm handclasp? We sometimes receive more help from faces than from words. God has ordained this blessed ministry of comradeship. Are you standing true to it?

Opposition—the Jews

Next the devil comes upon the scene. The new inspiration with which Paul had been baptized was met by a countermove of the adversary. "The Jews opposed Paul and became abusive" (18:6). Speaking of them in his letter at this time from Corinth, he refers to them as those

> who killed the Lord Jesus and the prophets and also drove us out. They displease God and are hostile to all men in their effort to keep us from speaking to the Gentiles so that they may be saved. In this way they always heap up their sins to the limit. The wrath of God has come upon them at last. (1 Thessalonians 2:15–16)

The situation now became impossible, and in the most solemn manner, as directly commanded by the Lord on such occasions, he shook his raiment and said unto them, "Your blood be on your own heads! I am clear of my responsibility. From now on I will go to the Gentiles" (Acts 18:6). The crisis had come. The Jews in Europe had rejected their Messiah as they had already done everywhere in Asia.

His Letter to the Thessalonians

He had written one epistle to the beloved disciples in Thessalonica, and soon after he adds his second; and now begins that marvelous ministry of the written epistle, and later the printed page which has created through the progress of Christian literature the largest pulpit and constituency in the world. There is no doubt that today the printed page reaches a far wider circle than even the spoken message, and that the Bible society is doing more, perhaps, to evangelize the world than even the multiplied voices of many thousands of missionaries.

One of the special features of this letter to Thessalonica was a request for prayer with which he closed his second epistle, "Finally, brothers, pray for us that the message of the Lord may spread rapidly and be honored, just as it was with you. And pray that we may be delivered from wicked and evil men" (2 Thessalonians 3:1–2). The rest of this chapter is a remarkable illustration of the way God answered this prayer.

Answered Prayer

1. First it was answered by the opening of a wider door at Corinth in the house of Justus, hard by the synagogue, where the two congregations doubtlessly met every Sabbath, and the Jews could see how God was blessing the apostle's work.

2. Next followed the conversion of Crispus, the chief ruler of the synagogue, and the most influential of the Jewish party. This was followed by many conversions, including well-known families, like the household of Stephanas, and Gaius, afterward so familiar a name in the writings of both

Paul and John. There was also a large number of the humbler classes, for, writing later to the Corinthians, the apostle reminds them, "Brothers, think of what you were when you were called. Not many of you were wise by human standards; not many were influential; not many were of noble birth" (1 Corinthians 1:26). There was another class whom Paul welcomed most gladly of all, that immoral and depraved multitude, the drunkard, the thief, the prostitute, of whom he says, "And that is what some of you were. But you were washed, you were sanctified, you were justified in the name of the Lord Jesus Christ and by the Spirit of our God" (6:11). So there came into the Corinthian church a blessed revival and a glorious company of ransomed sinners.

3. The next answer was a voice from heaven. Paul no doubt had been deeply discouraged by the opposition of the Jews, and affected still more by the painful stand which he had taken in withdrawing from the synagogue. Was he justified in this? The Lord saw that he needed the reassuring word, and how sweetly it now came and moored his tossing ship to the throne with an anchorage that would hold amid all the testings of the coming years. "Do not be afraid," the Master says, "keep on speaking, do not be silent. For I am with you, and no one is going to attack and harm you, because I have many people in this city" (Acts 18:9–10).

4. Next came the open assault of his enemies and their ignominious defeat. At this time a new governor had come to Corinth in charge of the

great province Achaia, of which it was the capital. It was Gallio, the brother of the famous philosopher, Seneca, who speaks of him in one of his writings as a man of high character and uprightness, and at the same time of easy indifference such as we see in his later treatment of the Jews at Corinth. Supposing that he would be ready to please their party by a little bit of favoritism, and at the same time, taking advantage of his supposed ignorance of the local situation, they summoned Paul from his tribunal under grave charges of promoting a new religion contrary to their law. Paul was about to answer for himself, when Gallio turned on the prosecutors and sharply rebuking their miserable quibbling about questions, about words and names and their own law, he nonsuited them. And as they still seem to have lingered and pressed the case upon him, he finally and evidently with some impatience "had them ejected from the court" (18:16). The mob waiting outside as usual to join the winning and fall on the losing side, immediately turned on Sosthenes, the chief prosecutor, and beat him before the judgment seat, while Gallio, true to the character that his brother had given him, "showed no concern whatever" (18:17).

Leaves Corinth

Finally the trial ended, Paul quietly settled down to a long season of successful work, planting numerous churches throughout Achaia and finding, it would seem, his sweetest revenge even in the conversion of Sosthenes himself, the leader of the mob that brought him before the tribunal of Gallio. We cannot, of course, demonstrate the fact that the Sosthenes who attacked Paul was the same Sosthenes whom Paul a little later, writing back from Philippi by the hand of Stephanas, associated with himself in his epistle to the Corinthians as "our brother Sosthenes" (1 Corinthians 1:1), but it does look as though he was drawing a very strong contrast between Sosthenes the bitter enemy and Sosthenes the now loving brother. May it not be that we shall some day find that as he lay there bleeding under the blows of the mob, Gallio caring not, and the crowd crying, "served him right," that Paul went up to him and kneeling by his side prayed him back to life, took him home under his loving care and won him to Christ? Surely that would be the most supreme triumph of faith and love.

Finally, we have not space to follow him as he closes his successful work in Corinth, sails across to Ephesus for a brief stay accompanied by Aquila and Priscilla and then presses on to Caesarea, Jerusalem and Antioch.

Close of Second Missionary Journey

As we thus close with him his second missionary journey, we cannot fail to note, first, the presence of the Master all through these missionary scenes, and the fact that He who "began to do and to teach" (Acts 1:1) is still continuing to work and lead his missionary army. Secondly, that the power promised at Pentecost is still the equipment and enduement of the militant Church—power to win souls, power to pray until both earth and heaven answer, power to hold back the hate of men and control the very officials in the judgment hall and power to build up and establish the Church of God in the face of the opposition of earth and hell.

Thirdly, we cannot fail to notice the ever-aggressive spirit of the gospel witness. Pressing forward from center to circumference, we still find it reaching out to the uttermost part of the earth. Rejected by the Jew it is given to the Greek, and now from its home in the continent of Asia we have seen it spreading over all the cities of Greece, and from the great commercial world-center of commerce, sending forth its influence through all the earth.

And last of all we have not only seen the splendid example of the great apostle to the Gentiles and felt our own lives dwarfed into littleness beside the grandeur of his life and work, but we have also seen that there is room for the humblest of his brethren by his side. If you cannot be a Paul in the pulpit, you can be an Aquila in the workshop and a Priscilla in the home. Or you can be a Timothy, bringing a word of cheer and the handclasp of comradeship to the tired worker. Or you can be a Thessalonian saint praying over yonder until it reaches both earth and heaven as it was so marvelously answered at Corinth. God help us so to help as in those days of old.

CHAPTER 7

PAUL AT EPHESUS

Did you receive the Holy Spirit when you believed? (Acts 19:2)
The word of the Lord spread widely and grew in power. (19:20)

These words reveal to us at once the secret and the story of one of the most glorious chapters in the life of Paul, the missionary. It is known as his third missionary journey. We left him closing his second journey at Jerusalem and Antioch, having called on his way home for a brief visit to Ephesus to prepare the way for his contemplated campaign and leave behind him Aquila and Priscilla to direct these preparations. His proposed visit to Ephesus had been divinely interrupted three or four years before in order that he might plant the gospel in Europe first. But now God's time has come, and the next three years find him in this splendid oriental metropolis and engaged in the most remarkable and successful of all his missions.

Ephesus

The city of Ephesus, the scene of his labors, was to Asia what Corinth was to Europe. They faced each other across the sea somewhat as Liverpool and New York, only while Corinth was marked by all the energy of the western world, Ephesus was a luxurious and splendid eastern city, and given up to the magic arts and idolatrous superstitions of the Orient. Its supreme glory was the temple of Diana, one of the seven wonders of the world. But the Diana of Ephesus was a wholly different character from the Diana of the Greeks. This famous temple covered a rectangle 425 feet by 225 feet. It was enclosed by a colonnade of 127 pillars, 60 feet in height and finely carved in the richest Ionic style. Unlike our sanctuaries, ancient temples were not roofed, so that most of the enclosed space was open to the sky, the shrine of the goddess being covered and more completely enclosed. A great number of eunuchs and priestesses ministered in its courts, and its worship and festivals were maintained by a number of distinguished and wealthy citizens called Asiarchs, or "chiefs of Asia," who met the expenses of these magnificent festive occasions from their personal means and counted it a distinguished honor to be permitted to do so.

To this great city Paul now came, not as he had wandered into Philippi, Athens and Corinth, a lonely stranger, but to find the hospitable home of Aquila and Priscilla awaiting him and his future work at least in some measure prepared.

But we are to look at this time at four pictures that stand out in bold relief from the story of his Ephesian ministry and speak to us lessons of peculiar appropriateness and practical power.

SECTION I—*Aquila and Priscilla: The Picture of a Home Missionary*

The story of a great life is sometimes discouraging because so few can reach the high station of a great apostle and missionary, but the Bible was written for humble disciples and everyday Christians, and the story of Paul is filled with innumerable side lights and companion pictures illustrating the infinite varieties and possibilities of Christian service. Among these no characters were more interesting than Aquila and Priscilla, whom we met in our last chapter at Corinth, and whom we meet again here and frequently afterward as Paul's friends and fellow workers. They could not be apostles, but they were indeed living "letter[s] . . . known and read by everybody" (2 Corinthians 3:2). Soon after coming to Ephesus they met with a distinguished and eloquent teacher and preacher from Alexandria named Apollos. Finely educated, mighty in the Scriptures and full of zeal and fervor, he had yet got no further than John's baptism and was eloquently preaching of a Messiah to come. With fine tact and wisdom they introduced themselves to him and took him to their home and lovingly led him into the deeper knowledge of the truth. Soon afterward he went over to Corinth and successfully continued the work which Paul had there begun, becoming in many respects as popular and successful as the great apostle himself.

The word used to describe the reception given by these good people to Apollos is a strong one, expressing cordiality and hospitality. They did not "go for him" as some modern Christians do for ministers with whom they may not agree, but they took him to them and by love and winning example quite as much as by wise teaching led him into the deeper life. There are today many ministers as defective and as sincere as Apollos, men that have never yet been brought into favorable conditions for seeing and receiving the fullness of spiritual truth. Their ministry would be multiplied in value a hundredfold if they would but receive the Holy Spirit. They cannot be argued into it. Controversy only antagonizes. They must be won. Oh, for the wise Aquilas and Priscillas that can love them into the better way! When the story of the most useful and successful life comes to be told in all its fullness, doubtless it will be found that some holy mother, some faithful teacher, some judicious friends, some silent personal influence was the factor behind their deeper experience and wider usefulness. The chief value of the Sunday school class is not even the Bible knowledge conveyed. Perhaps there is even too much of the normal mechanical element about our Christian work today, but it is the strong and con-

stant personal influence of a holy woman or a
godly man upon the young minds and hearts under their care, and who perhaps have no other
Christian friend on earth. Some of us remember
our early teachers and the veneration and emula-
tion with which we regarded and copied them.
Oh, mothers, teachers, Christian friends, do not
wait and wonder till some great occasion comes,
but meet the simple opportunities of life and pass
on the ministry of Aquila and Priscilla to the end
of the history of the Church.

SECTION II—*The Holy Spirit: The Picture of a Whole Gospel*

The incident of Apollos naturally introduces the
next scene at Ephesus and teaches the same spiritual
lesson. On arriving there Paul found a number of
disciples, perhaps from the congregation of Apollos,
who, like that teacher, had got no farther than John's
baptism. In answer to the inquiry "Did you receive
the Holy Spirit when you believed?" (Acts 19:2),
they astonished him by telling him, "No, we have
not even heard that there is a Holy Spirit" (19:2).
The apostle then instructed them in the gospel of
Christ and immediately on their baptism they received the gift of Pentecost, and from this new
Spirit-filled company the work in Ephesus began.
That is the right and only place to begin any deep
spiritual movement.

The condition of these Ephesian disciples is, we
fear, representative of a great majority of professing

Christians today. They have accepted the ministry of repentance. They have experienced to some extent conversion. They have begun to "quit their meanness" and change their course of life. But they do not know Christ as a personal and abiding presence. They have not received the Holy Spirit. They make no claim to sanctification, and, indeed, rather criticize and repudiate it as something for people that are inclined that way. And they hold themselves in some measure free to live a worldly and imperfect life because of the lower plane on which they are content to remain. Unfortunately many of their teachers are little farther on themselves. It is to these that God is sending home the question of our text, "Did you receive the Holy Spirit when you believed?" (19:2).

And this question is supreme. It was supreme in the life of the Master, for He did not begin His public ministry until on the banks of the Jordan He had made the full consecration of His life and received the descending Paraclete. It was supreme in the lives of the apostles. They were not permitted to go forth and begin their ministry, notwithstanding their long acquaintance with Christ and their undoubted conversion, until they had tarried at Jerusalem for the power from on high. It was supreme in the early Church and in her message to her first converts. "Repent and be baptized . . . in the name of Jesus Christ for the forgiveness of your sins" was their first message, but immediately it was followed by the rest, "And you will receive the gift of the Holy Spirit. The promise is for you and your children and for all who are far off—for all whom the Lord our God will call" (2:38–39). It is the heritage of the whole Church of Christ and none can be excused from it.

Beloved, have you asked to be excused? Have you received the Holy Spirit since you believed? Have you had as a definite experience the baptism of the Spirit? Is Christ to you a living constant reality? It is this that gives holiness. It is this that brings rest. It is this which fills the heart with victorious joy. It is this which heals and keeps the body. It is this which brings love, patience and sweetness of spirit. This alone can give you victory. Without this you are powerless to pray, to witness, to work for Christ. This is your panoply and equipment for warfare and work, and this is awaiting every willing and earnest heart. If you really want Him more than anything else you will not be long in finding Him. He will meet you on the way. He will lead you all the way. He will bring you to Himself and abide with you forever.

SECTION III—*Revival: The Picture of a Mighty Spiritual Movement*

With this deep spiritual beginning the work moved on, and soon we are in the midst of an extraordinary revival.

Preaching in the Synagogue

1. It commences in the synagogue, and for three months the apostle preaches to his Jewish breth-

ren and others concerning the kingdom of God. The best evidence of the power of the work is the anger with which many of the Jews turned against him and openly denounced him before the multitude, and then the usual crisis comes and he withdraws.

In the School of Tyrannus

2. The next phase of the work is in the school or academy of a prominent teacher named Tyrannus, where for two years the apostle is hospitably received and continues his teaching until this strong language was employed concerning the spread of the movement, "All the Jews and Greeks who lived in the province of Asia heard the word of the Lord" (19:10). There must have been a constant concourse from the city and province and a ceaseless ministry of teaching and preaching, excepting only the hours of toil which Paul always spent in laboring with his hands and thus ministering to his necessities and those that were with him.

Supernatural Signs

3. His ministry in Ephesus was now marked by a peculiar dispensation of divine healing. The spirit of power so rested upon Paul that something occurred which was unusual even for him. The very handkerchiefs which he touched were laid upon the sick and they recovered. This and a similar statement about Peter should not be twisted into an authorization of the fantastic claims of some modern teachers and workers. This is the

peculiar method of spiritualism, and we should be most guarded in anything that approximates to it. But in the case of Paul at Ephesus there had been special claims made for heathen magic, and especially the images of Diana and the mystic inscriptions upon them were supposed to possess a healing charm. Therefore God met this thing once for all on its own ground, even as Moses met the magicians of Egypt in order to show the genuine and the false. We will find that in the story of early Christianity special manifestations of divine healing accompanied special advances into new territory. While the ordinary operation of the Lord's healing is uniform and constant in the Church, the miraculous features seem to be intended as special signs to call attention to the truth and the gospel under circumstances where the divine seal is called for, for a time.

Satan Defeated

4. In connection with this a signal victory over the devil is brought to pass. Seven young pretenders, the sons of a priest, possessed of a reckless ambition to imitate Paul, attempted to cast the evil spirit out of a possessed victim. But to their amazement the evil spirit turned upon them and, repudiating their pretended powers, cried out, "Jesus I know, and I know about Paul, but who are you?" (19:15). And then the possessed man leaped upon them and beat them within an inch of their lives, until they were glad to fly from the place naked, wounded and half dead. An incident so dra-

matic and even ludicrous as this was sure to take the popular fancy and spread like wildfire over the city. No better vindication of Paul could have happened. The people were profoundly impressed, and even those that had been hesitating or compromising were brought to deep conviction.

Confession

5. This was immediately followed by a remarkable and public confession on the part of a number of professed believers who up to that time had accepted the new faith, but had still held on to some of their old idolatrous traditions and practices. Filled with awe when they saw the power of God upon the wicked men that had tried to imitate the apostles, they became convicted of their hypocrisy and were led to make a complete renunciation and bring their books to a public bonfire, so that from day to day, as the Greek term implies, the spectacle was presented of one after another bringing these mystical volumes and throwing them into the fire with humble and probably tearful confession of their wrongdoing. Ancient books were 10 times as costly as our literature, and the destruction of a library involved a large part of one's fortune. The total value of these books is given by Luke as an intimation of the stupendous importance and extent of this breaking down of idolatry. If we count these coins in Greek figures the amount was nearly $10,000. If the pieces of silver were Hebrew shekels it would be $35,000. Either

sum is large enough to show the fruits of a revival that can bear comparison with any similar movement in the history of the Church.

Trade Riot

6. We next find the power of this movement expressed in a business way. It literally broke down one of the industrial trades of Ephesus and caused a trade riot on the part of the silversmiths who had made their living by manufacturing silver shrines or little models of the goddess Diana for sale. These men came together under excited leaders—and a great concourse assembled in the theater where political assemblies were held, until the peace and safety of the town were threatened—denouncing Paul for having destroyed their business and challenged the very existence of the worship of Diana. A gospel that goes down to the heart of Wall Street and turns business upside down must have some power in it. Would to God that the gospel of today might strike our crooked financial schemes, our reckless speculations, our dishonest methods, and bring to confusion the mammon worship of New York as surely as the Diana worship of Ephesus.

The Chiefs of Asia

7. But even this was not so significant as the spirit of sympathy with the apostle which it brought out from the leading citizens of Ephesus. When Paul with his usual nobility and self-sacrifice was about to rush into the theater to save his

friends from suffering on his account, the very rulers of the temple already spoken of by us as the Asiarchs, or "chiefs of Asia," were the men who acted as his friends and begged him not to expose himself to danger. The gospel had reached even these men that were the official protectors and supporters of the worship of Diana. A little later we find even the town clerk himself tactfully taking the part of Paul, dismissing the mob with the official assurance that these men had broken no law, and anyhow whatever complaint was held against them should be presented in the lawful assembly and not made the occasion for a disgraceful mob which threatened to bring down the Roman army in one of its usual demonstrations upon them.

These are some of the signs on the surface of events which showed the tremendous power of the religious current that for the time had carried all before it in the old capital of the East.

SECTION IV—*Worldwide Evangelism: The Picture of a Mightier Ambition*

But not all this could satisfy the heart of Paul or turn him aside from his grander ambition to carry the gospel to the uttermost part of the earth. It was at this very time that there rose before his mind the supreme conception of one more advance movement upon the heathen world destined to capture Rome itself, the capital of universal paganism. Here again we see the same aggressive mission of the Church breaking through every obstacle and hindrance. Just as the Church had to be driven out by persecution from her first home in Jerusalem until "those who had been scattered preached the word wherever they went" (8:4); just as Philip was hurried on from the great revival in Samaria to meet in a desert the heathenism of Africa in the person of the Ethiopian eunuch; just as Peter was pressed beyond his Jewish conservatism and compelled to go to Caesarea, the Roman capital, and begin the great work of Gentile missions; just as the center of apostolic Christianity was removed in due time from Jerusalem to Antioch and the first missionaries sent out from that church, and just as a few years before this present story Paul himself had been pushed out of Asia, forbidden to come to Ephesus and compelled to go across to Macedonia to a more remote heathen world; so now the ever-irrepressible forward movement reaches on even to Rome itself, and neither his affection for his Philippian friends, his interest in the splendid work at Corinth, nor his magnificent success in Ephesus can interrupt the supreme necessity that is laid upon him to go into the very heart of heathenism, Rome itself.

"I must visit Rome" (19:21), is strong language for mortal man, but there is a must in every divine calling. There is a resistless impulse. There is a conscious heavenly calling. There is the faith of a mighty destiny beckoning us on and assuring us of victory. The missionary calling is always a supreme one: "I am compelled to preach. Woe to me if I do not preach the gospel!" (1 Corinthians 9:16). Oh, that God would put this *must* upon some heart that reads these lines!

The reason his strong language was not presumptuous was because he purposed it in the Spirit. It is right sometimes to have such purposes and plans. The Holy Spirit does not always lead us a moment at a time, but gives us far-reaching visions for faith, hope and holy service. Such purposes, when in the Spirit, will stand the tests that came to Paul—the mob at Jerusalem, the prison at Caesarea, the storm on the Adriatic, the viper at Malta, and even the warnings and entreaties of the too-fond friends that begged him to desist from that purpose for the sake of his own life and usefulness—none of these things moved him, but on to the end he followed that purpose and saw it all fulfilled.

The mighty mechanical forces which are driving our factories, our locomotives and our swift ocean racers are not of recent origin. Were I to ask you where this power comes from, of course you would say, "Coal." But where did the coal come from? Perhaps you would answer, "From the mine." But where did the mine come from? Ah, that is an ancient story. Ages ago yonder sun flashed down upon one of the tropical forests of ancient geological periods a consuming flame, burned it up and turned it into coal and packed it away by no human hand in those great depositories in the rock-ribbed mountains where today men find their coal. And so, God comes in some early period of a Christian life and there falls from heaven the fire of the Holy Spirit upon some chosen heart and life, and a mighty call, a heavenly purpose, a divine ambition and a supernatural enabling are granted to that life hidden away perhaps for years under the discipline of God's providence. But when God's hour strikes, the power is there, the instrument is ready, the missionary comes to the front, and that silent purpose is wrought out in living characters of mighty and everlasting blessing. Oh, that that purpose might rise today in some of your hearts! Oh, that that fire might fall, and the brief and coming years which precede the consummation might see it as divinely fulfilled as in the story of Paul and Rome!

CHAPTER 8

ON TO JERUSALEM
AND ROME

After all this had happened, Paul decided to go to Jerusalem, passing through Macedonia and Achaia. "After I have been there," he said, "I must visit Rome also." (Acts 19:21)

Then Paul answered, "Why are you weeping and breaking my heart? I am ready not only to be bound, but also to die in Jerusalem for the name of the Lord Jesus." (21:13)

The following night the Lord stood near Paul and said, "Take courage! As you have testified about me in Jerusalem, so you must also testify in Rome." (23:11)

Our survey of the life of the great apostolic missionary leads us at this time through the fair isles of Greece where many an excursion party is sailing at this time of the year on voyages of pleasure and study. Had we voyaged through these isles in the time of Paul we should have beheld many a magnificent city where today the

113

traveler finds but broken columns and buried ruins on shores of desolation. The temple of Diana and Colossus of Rhodes, the splendid amphitheaters of Assos and Mitylene, and the walls and palaces of Troas, are all since gone, but Paul remains a loftier, nobler figure today than 1,800 years ago. The only thing that is immortal is that which has been touched by the name of Jesus and the glory of consecration to His cross. Our survey at this time will take us through a swiftly passing panorama of vivid scenes, on each of which we can only pause to glance for a few moments.

His Plan

1. Months before, this journey had been mapped out in conference with the Holy Spirit, and Paul had "decided" (19:21) to pass on even from the thrilling scenes of his ministry in Greece and Ephesus to the two supreme goals that yet awaited him, Jerusalem and Rome. Deeper than any other feeling upon his heart, except the love of Jesus, was his devotion to his own countrymen and his desire to present to them the testimony of Jesus. Writing about this time his great Epistle to the Romans, we find him exclaiming,

> Brothers, my heart's desire and prayer to God for the Israelites is that they may be saved. . . . For I could wish that I myself were cursed and cut off from Christ for the sake of my brothers, those of my own race. (Romans 10:1; 9:3)

And now the time had come, so intensely interesting to him, so solemn and momentous to them, when he would give them the last message of mercy and the last opportunity of receiving at length the Savior they had so long rejected. Then it was Rome, the world's great capital, the citadel of Satan, the center of organized heathenism. No grander ambition had ever fired a human soul than the sublime purpose with which Paul now pressed on to the supreme achievements of his life.

Preparations for His Great Campaign

2. The first preparation was the revisiting of the churches in Greece. It might be long ere he should see them again. Indeed, the presentiment was upon his heart that he should see their faces no more. And so he makes a prolonged pastoral visitation of Corinth and the churches of Macedonia, sending all his companions but Luke forward to Troas while he lingers a little longer among his cherished friends at Philippi. In view of his going to Rome, he takes occasion while at Corinth to write his great epistle to the Roman church, in which he tells them of the deep desire that he has long cherished to visit them and his earnest prayers that "now at last by God's will the way may be opened for me to come to you" (1:10), adding,

> I long to see you so that I may impart to you some spiritual gift to make you strong— that is, that you and I may be mutually en-

couraged by each other's faith . . . I am so
eager to preach the gospel also to you who
are at Rome. (1:11–12, 15)

The Departure from Troas

3. Seven centuries before, a little colony had left
this same city of Troy, as told by Virgil in the famous story of the Aeneid, to found the great city
of Rome. Now another colony was leaving the
same Troy to win this very Rome for the kingdom
of Christ. It was a curious and appropriate coinci-
dence. But how much greater in its consequence
the present departure than even the story of Virgil.

A Memorable Sabbath

4. It is significant that the party waited at Troas
seven days in order that they might meet the
brethren at their stated service on the Lord's day.
They had probably arrived just after the Sabbath,
and so they tarried nearly a week for this purpose.
What a significance it gives to the Christian Sabbath, that eager as the apostle was to reach Jerusalem in time for Pentecost, yet he tarried a whole
week in order to have the privilege of joining in
the Sabbath services of the brethren at Troas. It is
evident that the congregation consisted of humble
working people who could not afford the time
from their daily toil, and therefore met at night.
The day began at 6 o'clock in the evening at the
close of the Jewish Sabbath. Paul's address would
doubtless commence soon after this hour, and we

are told that it continued long, even into midnight. The evening was hot, for it was the beginning of summer. The hall was lighted with many lamps; the air was heavy and the service was long. Quite naturally, one of the congregation fell asleep, and suddenly fell from the window upon the pavement below and was picked up dead. It is a little singular that Luke was not sent for, but Paul. Very quietly and unostentatiously the story is told of that marvelous miracle, how the apostle fell upon the lifeless corpse, embracing him and claiming his life from God, and then in the most unostentatious way quieting the tumult of the people and telling them that "He's alive!" (Acts 20:10). And then the service quietly proceeds as though nothing had happened, and the narrator does not turn aside to paint in sensational or glowing colors the wonderful miracle that stands beside the mightiest achievement of ancient prophets. It is evident that the Lord's Supper was administered at the same time. The service proceeded during the whole of that memorable night, and the awful shadow that had for a moment fallen was turned into unspeakable joy and praise, and an impression left behind that many a generation would doubtless retain in the early Church.

A Memorable Journey

5. Next morning the rest of the party embarked on their little ship at Troas, but Paul chose to remain a few hours longer and walk to the next station, about 20 miles south, there join-

ing the ship again. His first reason probably was that he might be a little longer with the disciples, might comfort some sorrowing hearts, might lead some inquirer to Christ, might finish some work already well begun which would have had to be neglected if he had hurried on with the ship. We can imagine the little company clinging to him, following him out of the town, walking by his side, one by one taking their leave with many tears, until, perhaps, one or two lingered still. Then the apostle was left alone to pursue his solitary walk that Monday morning along the old Roman road that looked upon the isles of the Aegean. What a light it sheds on the apostle's missionary methods! How often was this his only way of transportation! No palace car to bear him on his missionary journeys; no chariot or beast of burden to convey him and his effects, but, like his Master, on foot, walking around the world with the message of love. What a picture of self-denial, simplicity and devout faithfulness for all other missionaries!

A Memorable Parting

6. Joining his friends and ship at Assos, they sailed past Ephesus, as Paul's haste to reach Jerusalem would not allow him to venture again amid the scenes of his longest ministry. But he sends for the elders of the church at Ephesus to meet him a few miles distant at the next port, Miletus, and there occurs that memorable leave-

taking, which has fixed the standard for every subsequent minister and flock so high as to put to shame most of his followers. First he reviews the past and reminds them of his labors, not only publicly, but from house to house, of his faithful preaching of the whole counsel of God, of his many tears and temptations and of his humble labors among them, supporting himself by his own hands and ministering to the needs of others. Next he forewarns them of their dangers from false teachers and deceivers from among themselves and solemnly commends them to God and the Word of His grace, which is able to build them up and give them an inheritance among all that are sanctified. And finally he forecasts his own future, telling of the bonds and afflictions that await him, but the immovable purpose and fearless courage with which he presses on to meet his future, intent on one thing only: "if only I may finish the race and complete the task the Lord Jesus has given me—the task of testifying to the gospel of God's grace" (20:24). The meeting closes with a touch of pathos, as he tells them that they shall see his face no more, and they kneel down together on the shore in parting prayer, falling upon his neck and kissing him with many a fond and reverent expression of their devoted love. In the second century there were doubtless men and women living who could tell how, when they were little boys and girls, they looked upon this touching scene, and had the hand of the venerable apostle laid upon their heads in blessing and farewell. Such a spectacle would be an inspiration and an anchorage for the faith and loyalty of the primitive Church, stronger than all the power of persecution.

A Hard Test

7. We pass many an interesting scene on their rapid voyage; the island of Cos, the seat of the great medical colleges of that age; Rhodes, with its immense commerce and famous Colossus; and Patara, a great emporium of trade, but now a neglected ruin. There they embarked in a Phoenician vessel, and sighting Cyprus after a two or three days' sail, they landed at the old city of Tyre, where their voyage ended, and whence they set out on foot to Caesarea and Jerusalem. Here again there is a stay of seven days, doubtless for the same reason as at Troas, and here there comes to Paul his first great trial of faith. The disciples at Tyre, we are told, "through the Spirit . . . urged Paul not to go on to Jerusalem" (21:4). This was not a mere personal appeal, but a prophetic message, and it must have been a severe trial of his faith; but we find him calmly moving on, unshaken even by these impressive messages. A severer trial comes to him at Caesarea, for there not only the brethren, but the prophet Agabus, recognized by all as one owned of God, actually bound himself with Paul's belt and told the apostle that so would he be bound at Jerusalem and delivered to the Gentiles. Then followed a universal appeal

from all of Paul's companions not to go to Jerusalem, but it only called forth a more decided resolve that nothing should hinder the sacred purpose to which God had called him. "Why," he answered, "are you weeping and breaking my heart? I am ready not only to be bound, but also to die in Jerusalem for the name of the Lord Jesus" (21:13). They seem to have at once accepted his conclusion as the higher will of God, and answering, "The Lord's will be done" (21:14), they henceforth stood with him for good or ill. Thus we see the apostle's leading by the Spirit apparently contradicted by another leading of the Spirit, and yet in the end we find his first leading was sustained, the second appearing to be only a test that brought out the more fully his fidelity to God in the commission already given him directly from the Holy Spirit.

At Jerusalem

8. Passing rapidly over the incidents of his journey to Jerusalem where he lodged with an old disciple of Cyprus, named Mnason, along with the other brethren, we find him paying his respects soon after to James, the head of the church at Jerusalem, and being cordially received by him and by the elders while he rehearsed to them the story of his ministry, and they accepted the testimony and glorified God. Doubtless, he also presented to them the valuable offerings that he had brought with him from the Asian and European Christians for the poor saints in Jerusalem. It was a joyful oc-

casion and demonstrated that the Church of Jesus Christ, whether Jew or Gentile, was at last really one.

An Ineffectual Compromise

9. But now we find the apostle entering into a step which, while cheerfully acceded to by him, really seems to have been one of those compromises which seldom or never does any good. Yielding to the advice of James and the brethren, he consented to take a step at Jerusalem which might have the effect of propitiating the evident prejudice of the Jews and convincing them that the stories about his disloyalty to the institutions of Moses were false. This expedient was that he should assume the expense of certain men who had a vow, and with them purify himself in the temple and perform the customary ceremonial rites in the sight of the people, so that they might all see that he was still a good and faithful Jew.

We cannot too highly commend the sweetness of Paul's spirit in consenting to this, although we need not be surprised to find that, like all such compromises, it failed. In the midst of the ceremonial rites incident to this vow, Paul was seen in the temple by some of the Jews of Asia who knew him abroad as a missionary to the Gentiles, and who now accused him of bringing Gentiles into the temple and openly defiling it. A riot ensued, during which Paul was violently attacked and almost torn to pieces by the mob, and only escaped through the Roman garrison of the Castle of Antonia, which stood at the corner of the temple court, who with the captain of the guard suddenly came upon the scene and rescued Paul from their murderous hands, supposing him to be some revolutionary fanatic.

A Last Appeal

10. At this point Paul saw an opportunity for his long-desired message to his countrymen and begged the captain to be permitted to address the mob. This was granted, and standing on the barracks' steps under guard of the soldiers, Paul beckoned with his hand, and in Hebrew language, which at once awakened their respectful attention, Paul began to address them. First he told them that he was a Jew like themselves, zealous for the law, brought up at the feet of Gamaliel, and bitterly persecuted the sect of the Christians. Then he told them of his sudden conversion in the midst of his persecuting hate, and how it was through a Jew at Damascus, the godly Ananias, "a devout observer of the law and highly respected by all the Jews living there" (22:12), he was led into the light in the early stages of his conversion and baptized in the name of Jesus. Then he told them how it became the longing desire of his heart to testify to his countrymen, and how the Lord Himself had sent him out of Jerusalem and given him the commission in this very temple years before: "Go; I will send you far away to the Gentiles" (22:21). So far they had listened respectfully, but that last word was too much. They suddenly broke into an

awful uproar, crying out that he was unfit to live, tearing off their garments, throwing dust into the air, and going through all the demonstrations of religious frenzy. His message to Israel had been given and rejected. That hour meant much more to Jerusalem than it did for him. Their turning away from that loving appeal was the last act but one in the tragedy that culminated in the awful story of the fall of Jerusalem and the burning of their temple. Again and again had mercy lingered and God prolonged Israel's day of grace, but at every step it became more and more apparent that the heart of the people was hopelessly hardened and they had been given over to the spirit of unbelief and the final rejection of their Messiah. The solemn inexorable wheels of destiny were rolling on, and in a few years more they would bring the Roman eagles, and that devoted city should sink in a cloud of blood and flame.

How solemn it is that as Jerusalem turns herself against the apostle and the Lord, Rome stands forward as his defender. It was Paul's citizenship that saved him now, and it was the Roman guard that stood between him and his own people. Henceforth Rome is to take the place of Jerusalem and the Gentiles would inherit the privileges of the Jew. How wonderfully God had prepared the way for the spread of His gospel by creating the very power of Roman law and citizenship, under which Paul now took refuge when about to be scourged by the chief captain as a preliminary investigation of this strange riot. Paul at once demanded his rights as a Roman citizen, and immediately we find how the shield of that citizenship was henceforth thrown open to him forbidding any indignity to his person, and finally giving him the right of direct appeal to Caesar himself, by means of which at length the way was open for his very journey to Rome.

A Divine Reassurance

11. The sudden and exciting events of these days must have left Paul's spirit in deep confusion and oppression. Especially the incidents of the following day must have been peculiarly trying to him. Brought before the Council or Sanhedrin of the Jews by the Roman authorities in order to find out what the real trouble was, Paul saw an opportunity of tactfully throwing a bone of contention between the two parties that composed the Council, the Sadducees and the Pharisees. He knew that they took direct issue on the doctrine of the resurrection, and seizing upon this as a pretext, he at once announced with singular shrewdness that it was for the hope of the resurrection that he was called in question that day. This was, indeed, strictly true in one sense, and yet in another it was an evasion, for while he held and taught the resurrection, there was no other common ground between him and the Pharisees. However, it availed for the present to start a wrangle between the two parties in the Council, which took sides immediately, until the quarrel became so bitter that the chief captain

had to remove Paul and close the Council in confusion.

That night as Paul lay in his dungeon, in the prison, many conflicting thoughts must have passed through his mind, and doubtless there came to him the temptation to question some of his leadings. Had not the prophets told him that he should not go to Jerusalem? Had he not forced his own will and wishes against the will of God, and had he, indeed, been quite straightforward in all this matter? Was his attitude in yielding to the compromise with James and the brethren independent? Was his plea in the Council perfectly candid or slightly evasive? And, perhaps, the brave heart began to question and to sink, as we have all done in such a trying hour. It was just then that his blessed Master came to the rescue, as He ever comes when we are overwhelmed and in perplexity, appearing to him as He had done a few times in the direct crisis hours of his life. He said, "Take courage! As you have testified about me in Jerusalem, so you must also testify in Rome" (23:11). How those words were linked in his memory with the days that followed, and through every dark night and troubled day, like a beacon light, would guide him on to his final goal, until at last he could say on the threshold of martyrdom at Rome, "I have finished the race, I have kept the faith" (2 Timothy 4:7).

Beloved, the Friend of Paul is still our Friend. The voice that spoke to him in the dark hour of trial is still ready to speak to us. He did not justify all that Paul had done; He simply passed over it with divine magnanimity. To Him of great importance was that Paul's heart was true. There might be errors of judgment, and there are ever such errors with us all, but the supreme question is, "Do you truly love me?" (John 21:15). Before that every other issue was passed over, and the Lord accepted His servant and stood back of him for good and ill until his life work should be finished. And so, as we close this rapid survey, above all other messages it speaks this to us: to have some great purpose for Him, and from Him to get our marching orders directly from the Commander, and then to press forward unhindered, whether by good or ill, undismayed by calamity, undiscouraged by even the counsels of the dearest friends, satisfied to know that He is leading, and that we have but one supreme purpose—to follow Him, to please Him, to trust Him, and have Him say at last, "Well done!" (Luke 19:17). If that is your purpose then you cannot fail. If you can go forth saying with this glorious pattern, "I consider my life worth nothing to me, if only I may finish the race and complete the task the Lord Jesus has given me" (Acts 20:24), then you may be sure that, like the great apostle, you shall ever hear Him saying what Jehovah said to Jacob: "I am with you. . . . I will not leave you until I have done what I have promised you" (Genesis 28:15).

CHAPTER 9

PAUL, THE PRISONER

As a prisoner for the Lord, then, I urge you to live a life worthy of the calling you have received. (Ephesians 4:1)

We have been looking at Paul, the missionary, in his devoted zeal and worldwide evangelism, and we have felt how all other lives and labors dwarfed in comparison with the splendid example of his character and achievements. Now we are to see him in a character much more difficult to sustain, and one where human character is much more likely to break down. Many a man who can stand the test of the most intense labor and even the severest suffering wholly fails when laid aside from active service and compelled to sit in inactivity or languish in prison. The bird that can soar above the clouds and stand the longest and strongest flights, pines away when compelled to languish in a cage and beat its helpless wings against its prison bars. For the next two years of his life Paul enters upon this new experience as a cap-

129

tive and a prisoner; but the grace of God in his marvelous life is equal to the strain. Looking over the walls of his prison and the heads of his enemies, he sees only the hand of God in his trial, and he signs himself, not the prisoner of Caesar, not the prisoner of Festus, nor the victim of the Sanhedrin, but "prisoner of Christ Jesus" (Ephesians 3:1). He recognizes the divine will and goodness even in this painful solitude of his cell, in the visits of his friends and in the very trial of his case before his judges as a new pulpit of service and a new place of testimony; and perhaps some of the most precious messages and fruitful ministries of his whole life came forth from the dark shadows of his captivity in Caesarea.

In this he was not alone. There was another prisoner of the Lord whose lips they silenced and whose life they shut up in Bedford jail; but John Bunyan could write from his gloomy cell, "I was at home to prison, and I sat down and wrote because joy did make me write." And so from that cell came forth the wondrous dream that has lighted up the whole pathway of the *Pilgrim's Progress* for many a child of God through all the years that have come and gone. Another sweet spirit, Madame Guyon, of France, spent many a day within prison walls, and like a caged bird which sings the sweeter for its confinement, her heavenly song has echoed beyond her dungeon walls and lighted up the desolation of drooping hearts with heavenly consolation.

True, indeed, it is that

> Stone walls cannot a prison make,
>   Nor iron bars a cage;
> His presence ev'n a cell can make
>   A holy heritage.

Let us take three looks at Paul's prison.

SECTION I—*A Providential Protection*

Roman Citizenship

When Jerusalem turned against Paul, Rome opened her doors for his refuge. Back of the story of his life, we see the mighty hand of God and the executive sovereignty of the ascended Christ over-ruling both the history of nations and the smallest incidents of human life for the interests of His cause and His children. The same power that raised up Babylon to punish Jerusalem for its former sins, and then raised up Persia to protect the exiles of Babylon a little later, in turn gave the sovereignty of the world to the Greek race, in order that that perfect language might be spread among the nations as a vehicle in which the gospel was to be given to the world. When the mission of Greece was completed, Rome was raised up to take its place and consolidate the government of the nations under one powerful organization, which afforded the largest facilities for universal travel and the spread of the gospel rapidly through the known world. Rome was the providential preparation of God for laying the foundation of Christianity. Roman citizenship was a panoply in every part of the world, protecting its possessor from assault and injury and giving him the right of way in every land. This was Paul's safeguard, and behind it he took refuge when his own countrymen sought his life. The fortress of Caesarea, therefore, became for the time being the shelter and home of the persecuted apostle, and the bulwark of Roman law and the right of his appeal to Caesar guarded him from any injustice either on the part of his Jewish enemies or the unprincipled Roman governors who were only too willing to please them by cowardly compromises.

Jewish Hate Foiled

But again we see the particular providence of God in discovering and revealing the wicked plot of the Jews to assassinate the apostle when they found themselves baffled in their legal prosecutions. We do not know who this nephew was that God raised up at the right moment to intercept their plotting and report the matter to Paul and the governor, but God knew all about him and had him there ready for the occasion, as He ever has His instruments ready. In the same way, many a time has He interposed by some trifling providence to save the lives of His servants. Once He caused a spider to weave its gossamer web over the entrance to a cave where a venerable Covenanter had taken refuge a few minutes before. The cruel soldiers, who would have pursued and searched the cave, when they saw the newly made spider's web, concluded that no one could have entered, and passed on. Once in answer to prayer He caused a Scotch mist to gather like a curtain over a valley where the Dragoons of Claverhouse were about to pounce upon a little company of Christians worshiping in their mountain conventicle, and lo! the pavilion of God was spread over them, rendering them invisible to their pursuers and enabling them in safety to escape. Once He sent a hen to lay her eggs in the loft where one of His servants was in hiding, and supplied him his daily food until he was able to escape to a place of security. So, still His hand is guarding us in all dangers, and His covenant fulfilled to those who are true to Him. "I am with you and will watch over you wherever you go. . . . I will not leave you until I have done what I have promised you" (Genesis 28:15).

SECTION II—*A Place of Persecution*

For while he was protected from their power, he was not free from their persecution, and so in a few days his enemies pursued him from Jerusalem to Caesarea, where the governor had removed him to prevent the assassins from carrying out their secret plot. They lose little time about it. Five days after the scene in the Sanhedrin, in which he had declared that he was called in question for the hope of the resurrection, we find them at the Roman capital ready to press their charges against him with their attorney, Mr. Tertullus, all primed for the attack, and an eager mob of Jews, including even the high priest and the elders, on hand to echo his charges. The speech of Tertullus is a good sample of plausible and dishonest pleading. He begins by the usual flattering exordium, to which no doubt, the keen Roman was well accustomed and knew how to estimate its value. He told him how happy they were under his benevolent government, while Felix knew in his heart that a very slight pronunciation would transform "lawyer" into "liar." He was well aware how odious both he and his government were to the Jewish authorities and people, and how gladly they would hurl them from power if they dared. Then Tertullus goes on with his case, and begins it, as weak cases generally begin, with a little cheap abuse, calling Paul a pestilent fellow; then he grows more serious and charges sedition, but ere long reaches the real point of the offense, which is that he is the leader of the sect of the Nazarenes. Then he launches out into a lot of lying, telling how they would have tried him according to their own law, had not the Roman governor violently taken him from their hands. Felix knew how false this was, and that instead of trying him, they were trying to kill him, and that the Roman captain had simply rescued him from murder at the hands of the mob and afterward defeated their plot to assassinate him by a band of cowardly cutthroats that had entered into a conspiracy with the very high priest himself that they should neither eat nor drink until they had slain Paul.

Paul's Defense

Paul's turn now comes, and his defense is in dignified contrast with the enemies'. There is not one word of weak adulation or praise for the governor, but a manly, courteous acknowledgment of his confidence in answering before him, simply because through his long residence as a governor he was enabled to have thorough knowledge of the whole matter. Then comes his plea, in which he denies the charges and defies the accusers to prove them. He shows that there has not been time for any seditious plot, for it is only 12 days since he arrived in Jerusalem and six of these have been spent under the guard of Roman soldiers.

During the immediately preceding days he challenges any of his enemies to prove that at any time he was found disputing or causing dissension or tumult of any kind either in the temple or in the city. He acknowledges having been found in the temple, purified in the usual way, but without any disorder or unbecoming act on his part, the only tumult having been caused by certain Jews of Asia who were noticeably absent, and who ought to have been here now if they had any accusation to bring against him. He declared that he has simply been worshiping God according to the law and the prophets which they also accept, and that the one issue raised when he stood before their Council was the resurrection of the dead, which the Pharisees themselves believed.

At the end of his defense Felix postponed his decision, but evidently showed his leaning toward Paul by ordering the centurion to give him liberty to see his friends at any time, and keep him in prison with the most moderate measure of restraint possible. A little later Felix intimated that he would look more fully into the matter, and the narrator hints that his secret motive was that he hoped to utilize this opportunity in some way to gain some personal advantage out of it for himself. So far as the prosecution was concerned, it had failed, and the next move of his enemies was, under some pretext of law, to have him sent back to Jerusalem for trial before the Council, in order that on the way he might be attacked and assassinated. This Paul defeated by refusing to go back to Jerusalem for retrial and appealing directly to Caesar, which was the only way apparent by which he could have been saved from a violent death.

SECTION III—*A Pulpit and Place of Holy Ministry*

We now come to the deeper purpose of Paul's imprisonment. When the Lord Jesus forewarned His disciples that they should be brought before kings and governors, He had added, "This will result in your being witnesses to them" (Luke

21:13). That is, He meant that their public trials should be an occasion for witnessing for Christ. And so we find the apostle and his brethren always looking beyond the mere temporary occasion of their trial, to the greater object of bearing testimony for Jesus. The time had now come when the apostle was to have the privilege of speaking for his Master before the rulers of the world. He was to begin with the Roman governors and the Jewish king, and later was to stand before Caesar himself, as a messenger of Jesus Christ. The first of these opportunities comes in a few days. Felix sends for Paul to make a statement concerning the faith in Christ in the presence of Drusilla, his Jewish wife, whose relations to her husband, by the way, were not altogether lawful and right. Paul rises to the occasion.

Paul and Felix

A little while ago we saw Paul standing before Felix. We are now to see Felix before Paul. The tables are turned and the Roman governor is the trembling prisoner at the bar—the bar of conscience, the bar of truth, the bar of God's judgment seat. A little hint is given to us of how Paul addressed himself on this occasion. "Paul discoursed on righteousness, self-control and the judgment to come" (Acts 24:25). He did not plead for himself, he did not denounce his enemies, he did not dogmatize about his opinions, he did not try to show his eloquence or learning; he went straight to the point. This was a case of conscience, a case of sin, a case where a soul was standing at the crossroads of life and the gates of decision. And so with inexorable logic, with deep solemnity, and, no doubt, with much tenderness, he reasoned about the very things which affected Felix and Drusilla most solemnly and immediately. He told them, no doubt, about the holiness of God, the necessity of righteousness, the awful penalty of sin, the wickedness of sensuality, immorality and intemperance, and the certainty and awfulness of the judgment to come. We have some examples in his epistles of such reasonings. We remember how he told the Romans that "all have sinned and fall short of the glory of God" (Romans 3:23), and that "every mouth may be silenced and the whole world held accountable to God" (3:19), and how "the wrath of God is being revealed from heaven against all the godlessness and wickedness of men" (1:18). We remember how he told the Galatians that "God cannot be mocked. A man reaps what he sows" (Galatians 6:7). Doubtless, in similar terms he pressed the charges home upon the guilty consciences of his hearers. Perhaps, the guilty woman flushed indignant under his keen home-thrusts, then hardened herself against his appeals, while her less skillful partner in sin was unable to conceal his deep and growing feeling, until his very frame gave evidence of the awful strain upon his soul, his knees smote together, his whole frame trembled with deep agitation, and arousing himself from an embarrassment which was becoming intolerable, curtly cut short the address and dismissed the preacher by the memorable words, "That's enough for now! You may leave. When I find it convenient, I will send for you" (Acts 24:25).

A Crisis

No wonder that this passage has become historical and this scene typical of many a decisive moment in other human lives. The sequel in the case of Felix is very sad. Luke tells us that he sent for Paul more than once afterward, and for two whole years kept him in prison until his own term of office closed, when he left him bound as a heritage for his successor. But Luke does not tell us that he ever trembled again or came near that decisive place where once for a moment he had stood at the gates of life. On the contrary, Luke tells us how an ignoble, mercenary spirit took possession of his hardened heart, and he held his prisoner for the base hope of getting some bribe from him or his friends for his release. Failing in this, at last, with shameful cruelty, Felix left Paul bound as a criminal after he himself had given him liberty, and thus witnessed to his innocence. That heart, for a moment touched and softened, grew only harder and more wicked when it turned from the light, until we have before us the spectacle of a soul going steadily down into ever deeper degradation and sin, until, as it passes from our view, it is given over past feeling to its sin and doom. May it be that in that first moment of feeling Felix came within reach of eternal life; that that was his day of visitation, his brief day of grace, and when he missed it by procrastination, not only did it never come again, but it left him a hardened heart and more hopeless future than if it had never come at all? Would that soul remember some day in eternal darkness, how once the angel of mercy had visited him, once the gates of light were open to him, once Jesus Christ had stood with pleading, loving and open arms to forgive even him, and by one act of procrastination he had forever closed the door and sealed his own wretched fate?

There are some tragedies that come suddenly, as when Herculaneum and Pompeii fell under the flames of Vesuvius, or some soul is stricken down in the blossom of its crime going quick to hell, as Dathan and Abiram of old (Numbers 16). But there are other tragedies more slow and yet more terrible. There is no lightning stroke of judgment; but little by little, moment by moment, the heart grows harder, the conscience more insensible, the life more depraved, the soul more incapable of feeling or repentance, like a man slowly sinking in the quicksand and dying before our eyes by inches and moments of horror. So Felix went back from the hour of opportunity, and so still men and women are missing their chance and losing their souls.

I remember a pathetic story once told me by a brother minister with tears and bitter sorrow. "Last night," he said, "one of my college friends came late to my study. We were boys together in Baltimore and close friends. One night we both knelt at the same altar, where I gave my heart to God and he refused to give his. We parted that night. Ever since my pathway has been up to God, his has been downward. Farther and farther we drifted apart, until I seldom met him, and always when I did, noticed that he was on the downward road. Last night he nearly broke my heart. He was a bloated drunkard. 'John,' he said, 'it is probably the last time I shall ever ask you. It is nearly over. One of these nights, perhaps tonight, I will drop in my tracks, and they will hustle my old bones to the Potters' Field. Don't talk to me about Christ and heaven. I know all about it. It is all gone'. I looked once in His face and turned away. 'It is not for me now. I haven't heart enough to want it; I have not soul enough to seek it. I am dying, spiritually, as well as physically, and I am almost dead now. All I want is one drink more, one dime more, one dime more, one more chance to forget my misery. I will not trouble you again. Just a dime, and good-bye forever.' " A few months later my friend told me that the poor waif had gone. A few weeks after that night he had been picked up on the street—an accident, a fall, perhaps a collision with a passing car had given him the finishing stroke and his own prophecy was fulfilled. Ah, that is sadder than the sudden stroke of judgment.

Beloved, if you would only realize that when you say "No" to Christ today, or even put Him off until tomorrow, it means for you a slowly hardening heart, a gradually lessening interest, the power to sin without compunction, to lie down and sleep without prayer or fear, and so on down until the last act of the tragedy and it is forever too late, and the awful lines once written by Dr. Alexander, of Princeton, are true:

There is a time, we know not when,
　A place, we know not where,
That marks the destiny of men,
　For glory or despair.

To pass that limit is to die,
　To die as if by stealth;
It may not dim the sparkling eye,
　Or pale the bloom of health.

He thinks, he feels that all is well,
　And every fear is calmed;
He wakes, he sleeps, he walks in hell,
　Not only doomed, but damned.

How long may we go on in sin?
　How soon will God depart?
While it is called today, repent,
　And harden not your heart.

Paul and Agrippa

One more opportunity came to Paul at Caesarea, and one more lesson has come down to us from his message. It is a lesson that deserves to stand beside his message to Felix. It was before Agrippa this time, with Festus the new governor. Agrippa was one of the kings of Herod's line, and his dominion lay east of the Jordan. As a distin-

guished visitor at Caesarea, he was invited with
the court to hear the famous prisoner. The occasion was most distinguished, the audience illustrious, and the message of Paul was worthy of the
circumstance. It was the longest testimony pub-
lished from his lips. It began with the story of his
early life, his loyalty to Judaism and the marvelous revelation of Jesus Christ on the way to Damascus that had made him a Christian. Then it
was followed by the modest confession of his high
calling to be a witness of Jesus, and his solemn
declaration that he had been faithful to the heavenly vision and had continued to this day witnessing both to the Jews and to the Gentiles the
message of his great commission, the substance of
which was as Moses and the prophets foretold,
"that the Christ would suffer and, as the first to
rise from the dead, would proclaim light to his
own people and to the Gentiles" (Acts 26:23).

We can imagine the impassioned tones and the
glowing fervor with which he must have poured
out this eloquent appeal. So intense was the excitement that Festus, the cool Roman, could not
stand it any longer, but called out, "You are out of
your mind, Paul! . . . Your great learning is driving you insane" (26:24). To Festus, like many cultured people today, any religious excitement is a
sign of lunacy. Even the old-fashioned Methodist
"Amen" has become unfashionable in modern
congregations. But Paul appeals from Festus to
Agrippa, to whom all these great religious facts are
not new. Seizing his opportunity Paul turns his

testimony into a personal message, and asks his hearer, "King Agrippa, do you believe the prophets? I know you do" (26:27). It is this which elicits from the king his cool, and perhaps ironical, reply, "Do you think that in such a short time you can persuade me to be a Christian?" (26:28).

Our version of this text probably does too much credit to Agrippa. It was probably meant as a somewhat scornful reminder that Paul considered him an easy subject. "Easily wouldst thou persuade me," or "by a very little wouldst thou persuade me to be a Christian," is the literal meaning of the original. Agrippa probably meant that he was not to be so easily persuaded to accept the new faith about which Paul was so enthusiastic; but as the passage has come to us and has spoken its message to millions of souls, it has a meaning well fitted to go along with the other lesson from the story of Felix. While that lesson warns us against the danger of procrastination, this one warns us equally against halfheartedness in our decision for Christ. A reservation is as fatal as a delay. "Now and fully all for Jesus, and all for Jesus now." That is the gospel message, that is the warning lesson of the story of Paul at Caesarea.

Surely we need go no further than to Paul's own life to see the grandeur and the value of uttermost decision. Look at the compromising halfhearted men before him, and think of where and what they are today. Look at him bound, shackled and imprisoned at their bar once, but today higher than the stars, brighter than the sun. Oh, how gladly would all the Caesars exchange places with Paul now. And what was the reason for the difference? The one was out and out, all and always for Christ; the other self-seeking, halfhearted, compromising and of the earth, earthly, and "the world and its desires pass away, but the man who does the will of God lives forever" (1 John 2:17). Is there any soul reading this message and committing the mistake of Felix and Agrippa? Not far from the kingdom of God, just one step between, and yet that one step is sufficient to separate you forever from Christ and happiness and heaven. May the Holy Spirit help you to give up the last reserve and come to Him today and forevermore.

CHAPTER 10

A VOYAGE AND ITS LESSONS

I planned many times to come to you (but have been prevented from doing so until now) in order that I might have a harvest among you, just as I have had among the other Gentiles. . . . That is why I am so eager to preach the gospel also to you who are at Rome. (Romans 1:13, 15)

We are to look this time at a missionary journey, perhaps the greatest ever made, whose expenses were paid by the Roman Empire, a journey in which a prisoner became himself the captain and the crew his converts, and a journey which became a sort of type of the whole missionary work and future history of the Church, and a pattern of the principles upon which God in the coming ages was to work out the evangelization of the world. We have already called attention to the fact that the book of Acts has no formal conclusion, but like a broken column, it closes in the very midst of the story and leaves the later ages of

Christianity to add the finishing chapters. The lessons of Paul's voyage, recorded so minutely in the 27th chapter of Acts, divide themselves into two groups.

SECTION I—*Lessons for the Future History of the Church*

The Church's Voyage

It has been pointed out by a discriminating writer, Professor Stiffler, that the stormy sea through which Paul had to pass to Rome is the type of this tempestuous world wherein the Church has to work out her mission and destiny like a ship sailing over storm-swept seas. It recalls the picture in the Gospels where the Master ascended the Mount to pray and left the disciples to battle with the storm on the Galilean lake, coming to them at length in the fourth watch of the morning walking upon the sea. So the little ship of the Church is struggling through the tempests of time, while the Master is praying beyond at God's right hand and coming soon in His blessed advent. Perhaps the same lesson was suggested by the later scene on the same Galilean Sea, when the Master stood on the shore and called to His struggling and disappointed disciples as they cast their fishing nets into the sea. In the present instance we see the Church represented by Paul's ship passing through the stormy deep to reach the goal. That goal is Rome, which represents the heathen world. That voyage stands for the Church's great mission to evangelize the world. Opposition of the most formidable kind from the hosts of earth and hell assails her at every point, but with God in command and faith at the helm she passes triumphantly to her goal, and adversaries and difficulties are only met to contribute to the final result. But even when Rome is reached and the message given, we find that it is the old story, "Some were convinced . . . but others would not believe" (Acts 28:24). The evangelization of the world is a very different thing from the conversion of the world. As in the case of Paul, so it is still true and will be to the end of the story, "Some were convinced . . . but others would not believe." We are sent to give the gospel as a witness and gather out a people for His name; but the conversion of the world as a universal fact will never come until He comes Himself to establish His kingdom of victorious power and universal righteousness and peace.

SECTION II—*Lessons for Our Individual Life*

Trial

1. Trial turned to opportunity.

The whole story of the apostle's life was one of uninterrupted trial, opposition and persecution. God might have made it different; but the way of difficulty was for the education of His servants and the introduction of His kingdom. The Master Himself had foretold that His disciples should be brought before kings and councils in the course of their ministry, but He had added, "This will result in your being witnesses to them" (Luke 21:13). And so they recognized every situation as just an opportunity to preach the gospel. Instead of looking at their side of the trial and planning for their defense and deliverance, their first thought was how this affected the cause of the Master and the work of their testimony.

What a difference it would make in our lives if we accustomed ourselves thus to look at our trials. Have you thought of it, that perhaps the difficulty with which you are now contending, the uncongenial people and uncomfortable surroundings that so distress and apparently hinder you, are just a providential pulpit and congregation which God has given you for the purpose of reaching people that you could reach in no other way, and teaching or learning lessons which could only thus be exemplified? Stop looking at your end of it, and begin to think what it means for your Master and your fellow men, and so your hardest trials will become your most precious opportunities. Paul's arrest at Jerusalem seemed unfortunate, but it gave him his long-desired opportunity of giving his testimony to his fellow countrymen on the Castle steps in the Temple Square. His detention at Caesarea for two years seemed like a fearful loss of time in his busy life, and yet it enabled him to preach the gospel to governors and kings who never could have listened to him otherwise. The plot of the Jews to assassinate him, which was most cruel and cowardly, and the injustice of the Romans in working into the hands of his enemies by threatening to send him back to Jerusalem for trial and thus putting him in the power of his assassins, forced him to make a direct appeal unto Caesar for his protection. This appeal made necessary his journey to Rome and provided the long sought opportunity for carrying the gospel to the great metropolis of the world. Even the shipwreck and the "northeaster" (27:14) had their place, for they brought Paul to the front with his victorious faith and his splendid example, winning for him the hearts of soldiers and sailors, and enabling him to show the power and faithfulness of God to that heathen multitude under the most impressive circumstances. So God is ever giving to us new opportunities even in dark disguises. Let us not fail to recognize them and use the opportunities His providence sends us.

Disobedience

2. Disobedience leading to danger.

It was not long until the first vivid lesson was painfully taught the class in which Paul was now to be the leader. Disregarding his prudent message advising them to remain and winter in the harbor of Lasea, the centurion and pilot and owner of the ship decided to venture forward to the Port of Phoenix. Deceived by the south wind, which blew softly, they determined to make the venture in spite of Paul's warning, so they cast loose from Lasea, and sailed along the coast of Crete toward their intended harbor. But soon the soft south wind was exchanged for the wild "northeaster," a cyclone sweeping across from the African desert at certain seasons, rendering navigation most perilous. They soon found themselves helpless in the fury of the storm and were driven before it for many days upon a sea of foam and under a starless sky. Soon they had to undergird the ship to keep her from falling to pieces, and throw overboard the heavy freight and even the tackling of the vessel. The end was soon in sight, and the story records it in a few unmistakable words: "we finally gave up all hope of being saved" (27:20). Then it was that Paul stepped forward and reminded them frankly of their presumption and folly in neglecting his warning. "Men, you should have taken my advice," he tells them, "not to sail from Crete; then you would have spared yourselves this damage and loss" (27:21).

Disobedience always leads to danger. The way of wrong is the way of peril; the way of transgressors is hard. God has said so, and you can never make it otherwise. Right is always safe and wrong is always perilous. You can no more make a crooked line straight than you can make a wrong act wise or happy in its final issue. Oh, that the young minds and hearts of this seductive age would learn and remember that it pays to be true, honest, upright and good, and that "the wages of sin is death" (Romans 6:23), and the fruit of iniquity is bitterness and sorrow. Must God teach you this by breaking your own heart and wrecking your life? Will you not learn it from the lessons of the past and the uniform story of His own faithful Word?

Divine Help

3. Mercy in emergency.

The world is willing to echo the lesson of warning. Its philosophy is full of the maxims of prudence and practical retribution, but the world utterly fails to provide a way of escape when the mischief has been done. There is the difference between Christianity and ethical systems. They can tell us when we are wrong, they can upbraid us for having disobeyed the law of righteousness, but they cannot remedy the wrong or save us out of the consequence of our own sin and folly. The poor Chinese man was right when he told his people how Confucius and Buddha had come to him in the pit into which he had fallen, and gave him the best advice, explaining just why he had fallen in through his own fault and telling him what to do if he ever got out, but passing on in cold neglect and leaving him to his fate; while Jesus of Nazareth, without a word of blame, leaped down into the mire, lifted him out of the quicksand, cleaned and clothed him, and then took him by the hand and led him all the way. That is the beauty and glory of the gospel of the grace of God. How finely we see it in the story of Paul's shipwreck! "You should have taken my advice," he says, "then you would have spared yourselves this damage and loss. But now I urge you to keep up your courage, because not one of you will be lost; only the ship will be destroyed" (Acts 27:21–22). Then Paul tells them of his God and His promise and his own confidence in that promise, and from that hour takes command, as the messenger of hope and cheer and the instrument of the great deliverance.

It is only when you are at the end of all earthly help and hope that you find God and learn real faith. There is no situation so desperate but God can help it if we only will let Him. Even Judas might have been saved if he had listened to the gentle appeal in that crisis hour: "Friend, why have you come?" (Matthew 26:50, margin). The difference between Judas and Peter was that Judas would not believe in the mercy of Christ, and Peter would. Oh, how many today are taking their lives in remorseful suicide just because they do not know the infinite tenderness, love and grace of this heavenly Friend! Let us tell them of Jesus, the Friend of the helpless, the Hope of forlorn, lost men and women. Is there anybody reading this message, given up by your friends, given up by yourself, with no light or hope or prospect? Oh, beloved, listen to One who says, "Thou hast destroyed thyself; but in me is thine help" (Hosea 13:9, KJV). God is ready to forgive and forget all the past and make all the present and the future right if you will but trust Him and let Him have you. All He wants is a man who has come to the end of himself and is willing to begin again with God. There is mercy for the worst emergency, for the worst man or woman. There is mercy this moment for you.

The Salt of the Earth

4. The secret of Paul's safety.

Why was it that Paul could offer such a hope and lead such a rescue? Why was it that other ships went down in that storm, and his company were all safely landed? Why is it that some carry charmed lives and are immortal in the face of danger, death and even despair? Paul tells the secret. Here it is: God, "whose I am and whom I serve" (Acts 27:23). Do you belong to God? Then you are His property and He must take care of His property. Are you serving Him? Then His work is more important than anything else in the world, and nothing can be allowed to hinder it. Consecration is the secret of faith, and a life that is all the Lord's is panoplied by omnipotence and protected by every angel in heaven and every force on earth. But there is another element of safety. "Last night an angel of . . . God . . . stood beside me and said, 'Do not be afraid, Paul. You must stand trial before Caesar' " (27:23–24).

That was one of God's "musts." Men sometimes have their "musts," but, oh, they are shattered like the ships they sail on by the buffeting waves. But God's "musts" always get through. If God has a purpose for you it must be fulfilled. If God has a plan for your life and you have accepted it and committed it to Him for execution, neither earth nor heaven nor hell can prevail against it. If God has sent you to India, China, Africa or even Tibet you must get there. Oh, to have such a "must" in our life! What invincible power, what momentous impulsive force it would give to us! What confidence it will afford our faith as we quietly lean back upon the everlasting arms and see God triumph!

I know a woman who was dying of consumption and given up by all physicians, when it was distinctly recalled to her mind that in her early girlhood she had consecrated herself as a missionary to India and God had entered into a covenant with her to send her to that land. This recollection took possession of her and became interwoven in her prayer and faith, until she felt she must not die until she had fulfilled her heavenly calling. Need we say that the cable held, the faith founded on God's "must" was stronger than the power of disease or the word of physicians. She came forth from the last stage of consumption restored to perfect health, went out to India, preached the gospel there for nearly 20 years, and is today a woman in the full vigor of life, so hardy and robust that one would never imagine that she had ever known the awful disease. Have you got any of God's "musts" in your life? Ask Him to give you something to do, to put a mission in your life and a "must" in your future, and then go forth invincible to be one of the eternal forces in the world.

Believing God

5. The power of faith, hope and cheerfulness.

"So keep up your courage, men, for I have faith in God that it will happen just as he told me" (27:25). That single verse is worth all the philosophy and poetry of the world's literature. What else could inspire such a scene as that tossing deck presented, with the man who had gone on board as a prisoner, standing in the midst of 276 desperate men and making them eat and drink in the teeth of the storm, and put their hearts and hands together to save the sinking ship simply at his command! Beloved, if you want to be a power in the world and have an influence over your fellowmen, give up your groaning, whining, fretting and complaining. Arise and shine! "Shake off your dust;/ . . . Free yourself from the chains on your neck" (Isaiah 52:2). Throw off your gloom, depression, despondency and foreboding, and clothe yourself with the sunshine of hope and cheer, and go forth among your fellowmen radiant as the spring, bright as the morning and helpful as the light. Let your face be an epistle of joy and hope, let your bearing and your step tell of victory and gladness, and let your life be an evangel of hope and inspiration in a world where there are enough tears and clouds, and where God has sent us to be the lights of the world and the comforters of the sorrowing.

A Sound Mind

6. Faith and common sense.

We have some fine examples in this story of the perfect harmony between the most sublime trust and the most severe practical wisdom. "Not one of you will be lost," was Paul's announcement. "I have faith in God that it will happen just as he told me" (Acts 27:22, 25). More explicit and unquestioning faith we could not find. But a little later we hear him saying, as the sailor crew were trying to escape and leave the ship and the soldiers to their fate, "Unless these men stay with the ship, you cannot be saved" (27:31). Here are the two horns of the dilemma, the two sides of the great question of God's purpose and man's responsibility, but a common sense faith can easily recognize them. The God that ordains the end also ordains the means to that end. Faith and obedience are but the two oars of the boat, the two hands that grasp the hand of omnipotence; and if we truly believe God for the promise, we shall as certainly obey Him with respect to the command. The faith, therefore, that lies down in indolent inertness and fails to watch and work in the line of God's plan and as the instrument for answering its own prayers, if such be God's way, is not intelligent, scriptural faith, but ignorant and foolish presumption. The man that pleases God always obeys God and watches and hearkens to know His will and to be used by Him in carrying out the promise on which that faith was supremely realized. God gives us wisdom to understand at once the confidence of faith, and, while we trust Him with all our heart, to obey Him with responsive feet and willing hands.

Hard Places

7. The value of hard places.

One has often been tempted to wonder why God allowed His distinguished servant to have so hard a struggle with the elements. Why did not some mighty angel come with a lifeboat from the skies to transport the great apostle through the surf and storm and let the world see how mighty was his God? Why did God allow him to drift for days in the tempest, and at last narrowly to escape like a waif flung ashore on a floating plank or fragment of the broken wreck? Oh, that is God's way of hiding His power and teaching us the lesson of true power ourselves. Only by the discipline of difficulty do we ever learn to put on His strength.

One day an amateur naturalist saw a butterfly struggling out of its cocoon or shell, and he thought he would help the little worm to liberty. So he gently cut a larger opening in the mouth of the shell, and the struggling worm found it easier to get out and duly emerged into the light and liberty of his new birth. But, alas, that worm never could fly. The others came out later with hard struggling through their narrow cells, and soon were beating the summer air with their buoyant wings. But this lazy grub lay around on the leaf in indolent apathy and sordid helplessness, and in a little while died of uselessness, while the others went forth into their heaven of summer glory, among the blossoms and the branches. Ah, dear friends, that is what would happen to us if God made it too easy for us. We would grovel on the ground and would be ruined by ease and self-indulgence. Let us thank Him for the wholesome discipline and the inexorable love that will not let us miss our life's lesson and our eternal recompense.

CHAPTER 11

PAUL AT ROME

And so we came to Rome. The brothers there had heard that we were coming, and they traveled as far as the Forum of Appius and the Three Taverns to meet us. At the sight of these men Paul thanked God and was encouraged. (Acts 28:14–15)

We left Paul swimming ashore on the coast of Malta on a piece of broken wreck, having saved the whole company and crew of the ship by his faith and courage, and doubtless having endeared himself to the hearts of all the 276 souls whom God had given to him. We now find him in the midst of a barbarous crowd of natives who received the refugees with rude hospitality and kindness. It was wet and cold, for it was now the depth of winter, probably the month of December, and the people kindled a fire on the shore and proceeded to minister to the comfort of their unexpected guests. Paul, just like himself, without waiting to be waited upon, went to work to help himself and his companions and began to gather sticks for the fire. Suddenly a viper sprang from the flames and seized upon his hand, and immediately the superstitious natives concluded that he must be some notorious criminal whom vengeance was pursuing; but when Paul quietly flung off the viper into the flames again, and instead of his hand swelling and some terrible fit seizing him, he appeared to suffer no harm, their suspicions were changed to superstitious awe, and they were ready to worship him as a god. At the same time an opportunity was afforded by the sickness in the home of Publius, the chief man of the island, for Paul to go to him and minister in the name of the Lord. The prayer of faith, and his healing in answer to prayer, produced a deeper impression upon the hearts of the people, so that from other parts of the island the sick were brought to him, and doubtless the good missionary took advantage of the opportunity to preach to them the gospel and turn to good account the three months they were compelled to linger on the island. On their departure they were loaded with gifts and honors, and no doubt, a blessed missionary work had been accomplished and a seeming calamity turned into a blessed opportunity.

Reaching Rome

With the opening of navigation early in March, a corn ship of Alexandria, which had wintered in the island and was on its way to Naples, took them on board and they resumed their journey. Calling at Syracuse, the principal city of Sicily, they tarried three days. Then, passing Rhegium, they entered the harbor of Naples and moored at the destination of the trade ship at the wharves of Puteoli. Here they found a little company of disciples with whom they tarried the usual seven days, waiting, no doubt, over the Lord's day. Their march was next resumed overland along the famous Appian Way toward Rome. This famous road had been trodden by mighty armies and famous travelers often before, but no such distinction ever came to it as when it was trodden by the feet of Paul on his way to Rome and martyrdom. About 30 miles from Rome there was a little station called the Forum of Appius, where an important crossroad struck the Appian Way, and here the first party of Christians in Rome had come out to meet and greet their venerable visitor. Ten miles nearer the city was another town known as the Three Taverns, also a junction with an important road and a place of public resort, and here the second party of his hosts and visitors were waiting. Less vigorous, perhaps, than the others, they had not been able to take the longer walk; but now all reunited, and as a joyous procession, walked back by his side under the escort of his Roman guard and entered Rome.

The city was at its best. Two million people crowded within its walls and overflowed its suburbs, covering every hillside with the villas of the wealthy, while the crossings of the great avenues and the many hills that covered the site of seven-hilled Rome were crowned with arches, monuments, palaces, public baths and imposing edifices. Paul's destination was the Praetorium, or barracks, near the imperial quarters in the Palatine Hill. Here he was delivered over by Julius, who had charge of his escort, to the captain of the guard, a distinguished Roman named Burrus, whose name has come down to us from contemporary Roman history as a worthy and upright man. For the present, Paul's trial was postponed until his accusers could come from Palestine with their witnesses. Meanwhile, he was treated with marked courtesy. While, of course, he was a public prisoner and never could be separated from the Roman soldier who was chained to his arm, yet he was allowed to live in his own private lodging and receive such friends as he chose to come to him, with perfect freedom. Just as soon as he had become settled in his lodgings and had had a brief rest from the fatigue of his journey, after three days he sent for the chief of the Jews and made an appointment for a meeting with his countrymen, that he might lay before them his message.

On the appointed day they came in great numbers, for Rome had then its Jewish quarter, even as it has today its famous ghetto, and they formed a distinct and important element in its population. It was a memorable day in the history of Israel. From morning until night Paul reasoned with them and laid before them the proofs of Christ's Messiahship from the Old Testament Scriptures, and when the day was over it was found that while some believed, many still refused to receive the message and the chief body of his people seemed to have not only left his apartment, but separated themselves from his fellowship; for the language employed denotes a formal and final separation, and Paul's solemn message to them as they left him leaves no doubt that he so understood it. Affectionately, but very solemnly, he applies to them the warning words of the prophet Isaiah, and formally turns from them to the Gentiles, declaring that to them the message now is sent and they will receive it.

Work At Rome

The two years that followed were filled with constant work on the part of the apostle. Many came to him and many we know became followers of Jesus, and the church in Rome grew in numbers and influence. The soldiers who successively guarded him became in turn the subjects of his prayers and his messages and his effectual influence, so that in writing to the Philippians, he could say that the things that had happened to him had turned out for the furtherance of the gospel, and that through all the barracks his bonds in Christ had been made manifest and his testimony honored of God. Writing from Rome he could send greetings to the distant churches from those that were of Caesar's household, and quote name after name that was remembered among the disciples of the Lord. The sequel of Paul's story is gathered from various sources, partly from his own later epistles, partly from ancient traditions and Church history. It seems to be beyond doubt that, shortly after the two years mentioned by Luke in Acts, his hearing before Nero occurred and he was acquitted and released. Then he returned to the West to preach the gospel in Spain, revisited his old churches in Greece and Asia Minor and was again arrested, sent to Rome for trial, condemned and finally beheaded about six years after this, probably in the year 68, just a little before the capture and fall of Jerusalem.

Lessons

But it is time to turn from the narrative of facts to spiritual facts and spiritual lessons to be gathered from these incidents and scenes.

1. Satan not only defeated, but turned into an ally.

The savage attack of that viper upon the hand of Paul was but a stroke from the old serpent, the devil, who employed him; but it reacted against its intended purpose, and when Paul was not only uninjured but victorious over its malignant power, it gave him double influence for God. So every blow of the devil may be turned to our own advantage, and God be glorified by the strange spectacle of even Satan being forced to be our ally and really help on the cause he hates. Let us not fear our conquering foes. Let us never forget this verse: "without being frightened in any way by those who oppose you. This is a sign to them that they will be destroyed, but that you will be saved—and that by God" (Philippians 1:28).

2. *Adjusting ourselves to our circumstances.*

How perfectly Paul fitted into the providential framework of his life. Put him on a storm-tossed vessel, or on a floating spar, or on a savage shore at Malta, or chain him to a Roman soldier in the Praetorium—he was equally at home in all. He did not quarrel with circumstances, but he adjusted himself to them and turned them to account. Look at him gathering sticks for that fire, with simple-hearted, unaffected freedom, helping to make himself and others comfortable, instead of complaining about the wet and cold. This is the true missionary spirit and this is the true secret of happiness and healthiness in every station in life.

3. *The immortality of goodness.*

The scenes through which Paul passed on his voyage to Rome have derived much celebrity from many distinguished names. But the name of Paul has given them a higher distinction than all the story of the Caesars. The very bay where his ship ran ashore is known today as St. Paul's Bay. The place where he landed at Naples has been sought throughout all the centuries by loving and admiring followers, ever since the day when old Ignatius tried to trace his every footstep along the Appian Way to Rome. And as the ages go by, every other memory will pass into oblivion; but the name, the words, the works of Paul will possess an interest and claim a love and veneration before which all other associations must pale.

4. *The rejection of Israel.*

No sadder, darker shadow falls upon this story than that last meeting of Paul with his countrymen at Rome. Could we but see its mournful issues as it must have impressed the heavenly beings, it could only seem unutterably sorrowful. It was the last opportunity of Israel. During his earthly ministry how often had the Master called them; then at Pentecost they had received the message once more, and again and again Paul himself had pleaded with them. His love was so deep that he could even almost wish himself accursed from Christ for his brethren according to the flesh. At Antioch he had pleaded with them once more, and then with deep sorrow had turned from them to the Gentiles. On the barracks steps at Jerusalem he had once more appealed to them and given them his own testimony and his Master's message, but they had rejected it and sought his very life, even as they had martyred Stephen because he had witnessed to them of the same hated name. One more opportunity, however, is afforded. As Israel has heard at Jerusalem, at Antioch and in all the synagogues of the world the message of her Messiah, she must hear it once more at Rome, but it is the old story. Again it is met by unbelief; and now the voice of mercy ends, the day of grace is over, the sentence is pronounced, the salvation of God is sent unto the

Gentiles and they will hear it, and Jerusalem is left to her fate. Already the Roman eagles are preparing to descend upon their prey; and ere many years have passed, the terrible presentiments will begin, the fluttering wings will be heard within that Holy Place, while voices murmur, "Let us depart," and Israel will be led forth "as prisoners to all the nations. Jerusalem will be trampled on by the Gentiles until the times of the Gentiles are fulfilled" (Luke 21:24). Paul's loving eyes and ears shall be spared the spectacle. He shall be with his Lord before the final tempest breaks, and almost as soon as his martyr spirit shall have reached the arms of Jesus, the fatal cordon will be fastened around Jerusalem and the day of her visitation will have begun.

Oh, that the children of the kingdom, who like Israel of old, are trifling with this great salvation and missing their birthright, even as Israel missed hers—oh, that they would remember the warning: "If God did not spare the natural branches, he will not spare you either" (Romans 11:21). Israel had her day of opportunity and grace. Christendom is having hers. Soon that, too, will close, and Israel's day may return once more. Let us learn the lesson of her rejection, and "Today, if you hear his voice,/ do not harden your hearts" (Hebrews 3:7–8).

5. *The open door of the Gentiles.*

"Therefore I want you to know that God's salvation has been sent to the Gentiles, and they will listen!" (Acts 28:28). As the door of grace for Israel closed, it opened for the Gentiles, and now it was fully opened. The gospel henceforth was to make rapid progress at Rome and throughout the Roman world, and the epistles of Paul written from Rome showed how rapid and substantial that progress was. In his own hired house he daily received inquirers, "Boldly and without hindrance he preached the kingdom of God and taught about the Lord Jesus Christ" (28:31). He wrote the epistles to the Ephesians, the Colossians, the Philippians and Philemon during these two years. Many in Caesar's household and many in the Roman Praetorium became followers of Jesus Christ, and from Rome, the center of the world, the light went forth among all nations. Paul himself a little later passed again over the familiar scenes of his former labors and went far beyond the old boundaries, even to distant Spain. And ever since, that door has been opened more and more widely, until today the gospel of the kingdom has been preached for a witness unto almost all nations, and the glorious work the apostle began is nearing its consummation. More widely than ever God has opened the last closed doors during the present generation, and now there is scarcely a region of the globe where the messenger of Christ may not enter, and where, indeed, the pioneers of the gospel have not already begun their final proclamation before the end shall come.

6. *A pattern missionary.*

The profoundest of all impressions that come to

us as we follow to its close the story of Paul is the character of the man himself. We have seen it in many lights. The last picture is one of exceeding brightness, helpfulness and suggestiveness. "Paul thanked God and was encouraged" (28:15). What a light it sheds on that glorious, radiant life! There at the gates of Rome, there on the threshold of the cruel Nero, there where he was to suffer and die, there is no shrinking; there is only gratitude and fortitude, thankfulness for the past, fearlessness for the future. "Paul thanked God and was encouraged"! There he stands waving the banner of victory for every succeeding soldier of the cross and begging us to follow in the path of trial and triumph with the same hopefulness and the same heroic courage.

Why did he thus thank God and take courage? First, because it was his spiritual temperament to be cheerful, hopeful and brave. Perhaps it was not his natural temperament; but Christian character does not come by birth, but by second birth. It is not our disposition, but Christ's disposition that should determine our spirit and character. And wherever the Holy Spirit dwells and Christ is enthroned, there must be the spirit of joy, of peace and of confidence. Next, it was the presence of his friends that cheered and inspired him. We know who some of these were. He had sent greeting to them in the 16th chapter of Romans. There were Aquilla and Priscilla, his oldest and perhaps his dearest friends; there was Mary, who bestowed much labor on him;

Tryphena and Tryphosa, who labored in the Lord, and the beloved Persis that labored much in the Lord. There, too, were Timothy and Mark, and other friends who had labored with him in Asia and in Greece. What a joy it must have been to meet them! How their coming seemed to him a signal and a token of blessing and victory! With what tears and smiles and handclasps they must have met and then journeyed on together side by side those 30 miles to Rome! Thank God for Christian friendship. Thank God for true laborers in Jesus Christ.

Thank God for the love that seeks not her own, and that brings with it a fresh touch of the love of the Master. Beloved, how shall you have that hallowed blessing which was so dear to Paul? Let us whisper the secret. It is a very important one, but a very simple one. It is this: Love your friends, not for your sake but for their own; not for what you can get out of them, but for what you can be to them in unselfish blessing. Is not this the trouble with many of you? Is not this the reason why you are so often complaining of slight and neglect? That very complaint shows that what you are thinking of most is your side of the friendship and how it affects you. Rather learn to think of it as it affects them and makes you a blessing rather than a subject of blessing, and be well assured that if God makes you a blessing to another life it must inevitably come back to you in return. Ask God to give you an unselfish interest in the joy of ministering to others and forgetting self in helping them. This is the love of God, and this is the love that God loves and blesses. Be well assured that this is the real cause of all your disappointments in Christian love and fellowship. Paul had not one selfish thought. He loved his friends as few men did. He could say to them that they were in his heart to live and die with them, and that from the very beginning of the gospel they all had been partakers of his grace. Night and day he prayed for them and carried their every burden. Was ever soul more enriched by the treasures of love and prayer? Look at them falling on his neck yonder on the shores of Miletus and by the ship as it sailed from Tyre. Look at them walking out 30 miles from Rome to meet him on his way. Was not that enough to repay a man for the toils and sacrifices of a lifetime? God give us the same spirit of helpful love!

Again, Paul thanked God and took courage because of the wonderful providences that had led him hitherto. How could he help thinking of all the way he had come, and the hand that had led him to this hour, and that, notwithstanding the appeals of friends, the threats of enemies and the hate of hell, kept him true to his purpose and carried him safe to his goal? But the deeper secret of Paul's courageous spirit was his confidence in God and his close union with the spirit of his Master. Writing from Rome about this time to the Philippians, and giving us a glimpse of his very heart, he gives utterance to the same spirit of trustfulness and victory. He says:

I have learned to be content whatever the circumstances. I know what it is to be in need, and I know what it is to have plenty. I have learned the secret of being content in any and every situation, whether well fed or hungry, whether living in plenty or in want. I can do everything through him who gives me strength. (Philippians 4:11–13)

That was the secret of it all—the Christ who was his strength, the Spirit of the Master, the indwelling presence of the Lord, the deep lessons that he had learned in the school and under the discipline of the Holy Spirit. Not always could he say this, but now at last he says, "I have been instructed, I have learned my lesson and it is settled."

Again Paul was cheerful and hopeful because he was about to begin his cherished lifework. He had longed for this open door. Now it had come and he was about to enter upon the supreme work of his life. How he had loved that work; how he had lived for it; how he devoted himself to it and buried every private interest and every personal aim in the one purpose, to witness to Jesus and glorify His name. This is the true missionary spirit, and with this we are ready for the hardest service or the homeliest trial.

The story is told of a missionary candidate who applied for appointment for service on the field. His case was referred to a wise old clergyman who was to examine him and report upon his case. The good minister invited him to call at his study on a certain morning, naming the hour at 3 o'clock in the morning. Of course, it was a most unusual hour, but true to his appointment the young man was there on time. The servant, duly instructed, met him at the door and showed him into the waiting room. There he sat until 8 o'clock in the morning, when the host received him without a word of explanation. He asked him a few very ordinary questions. Among other things he inquired if he had a good English education, had studied grammar, could spell correctly and finally wound up the humiliating examination by asking him if he could spell the word "fox." This was duly done, and then he asked him if he had studied arithmetic, and this examination closed by a sum in addition, consisting of the two figures, 2 and 2 are 4. The young man meekly answered every question and was duly dismissed and told that was all. He went away wondering whether he had been taken for a fool, but in due time he received word that his examiner had reported very favorably upon him and that he had been accepted. The report of the old gentleman was something like this:

"I have examined Mr. So-and-So, and I consider him well fitted for missionary work. In the first place I examined him in punctuality, and I found that when I invited him to call at 3 o'clock in the morning he was there on the minute. Next I examined him on humility, and I found him to be proficient there, for when I asked him questions that any infant might have answered, he answered them meekly without asking any questions. I examined him in patience, gentleness, meekness and love, and I found him equal to the test. He waited for five hours for my coming to receive him, but he made no complaint. He must have been perplexed at the way I examined him, but he showed no trace of irritation. His whole spirit seemed to be under the control of Christ, and I have much pleasure in recommending him as a graduate in the school of his Master, and a worthy witness for His name."

Whether the incident is true or not, the lesson is, beyond all question; and happy would it be for many a missionary, more proficient, perhaps, in the culture and theology, if they could meet the same tests of all those spiritual qualities which constitute the testimony of our lives, and the absence of which will surely defeat all our words and works. While we thank God for the glorious achievements of the great apostle, while we look with wonder and amazement at his labors and sufferings, greater than all is his life and character, and best of all his testimonies is this: that he could say, "Follow my example, as I follow the example of Christ" (1 Corinthians 11:1).